BoomerPreneurs

How Baby Boomers Can Start Their Own Business, Make Money and Enjoy Life

M. B. IZARD

A **personal coaching approach**
to business start-up

Ideal for:
retirees, soon-to-be retirees, displaced workers, the unretired and those who always dreamed of having their own business

ACHĒVE
consultinginc. | 913-522-6184 | consultACH.com

Published by Achēve Consulting Inc.

913-522-6184

www.consultACH.com

Printed in the United States of America

This book is written to guide Baby Boomers in the entrepreneurial planning process. In this book, the author and publisher are not engaged in
rendering accounting, legal or other professional advice and services.
This book is sold with the understanding that the reader will not interpret the information included as such. It is recommended that the reader
check with the appropriate experts, such as a qualified attorney or an
accountant, for specific answers or for professional services.
Throughout the book, numerous Web sites are identified. This is not to
be construed as endorsements of the specific Web sites or organizations.

ISBN 978-0-9728748-3-0

V.1.1

Why This Book Was Written

After years of working with aspiring entrepreneurs on the business planning process—how to write a business plan and launch their businesses—it became apparent to me that much time and energy can be saved by expending more effort on the front end. That is, identifying business ideas that fit entrepreneurs needs and goals, evaluating and refining their ideas and then planning prior to moving forward. Many times the business ideas that individuals have do not mesh with their plans and dreams for the future or utilize their skills. In addition, the market viability of their idea is often an afterthought.

Baby Boomers have even more challenges than their younger counterparts, as at 50-plus years of age they are dealing with issues of aging and how to pursue their entrepreneurial dreams without risking funds earmarked for retirement or their children's college education. Faced with these realities, many individuals abandon the pursuit of their entrepreneurial dreams or, if they persevere in launching their businesses, are saddled with business demands that are not conducive to the lifestyle they desire and the future they envision for themselves. With careful planning, these issues could be avoided.

This book was written to fill this planning gap—to guide aspiring entrepreneurs through the process of selecting businesses that fit both their own needs and those of the marketplace—and to assist them in successfully launching their businesses.

Acknowledgments

I am most appreciative of my peers and colleagues who have supported my entrepreneurial interests over the years and, in particular, those who worked with me on developing this book. These include my awesome content review team—Kathy Nadlman, Donna Duffey, Cheri Streeter and Barbara Cunningham, all experts in the field of entrepreneurship. I am also indebted to Ken Gibson, whose initial feedback on my writing style was invaluable, and the members of my Book club, Diane James, Mary Sue Long, Bitsy Sader and Karen Bullard, who were a sounding board and provided my first reviews.

I'd also like to thank Julie Haas, who helped me name this book and all of those who helped me identify entrepreneurs to include in it—members of my content review team as well as entrepreneurship center directors Diane Sabato, Malinda Bryan-Smith, Tim Mittan, Mary Lea Dixon and Ginny Robert. I apologize in advance if I have left out anyone's name.

Next I want to thank my husband Jack, daughters, Brooke and Blair, and family and friends who patiently listened to me talk about writing this book for the last year and a half. And finally a special thanks to Pola Firestone, Kirsten McBride and Greg Gildersleeve for their editing and technical expertise and Gwyn Kennedy Snider for the wonderful book cover and layout.

I would also like to thank the hundreds of present and future entrepreneurs I have met over the years who have made my work both exciting and rewarding.

Table of Contents

Introduction

This is a book that can open up new possibilities for your future—that of owning your own business. Regardless of your motivation—planning for retirement, already retired, displaced from a job or fulfilling a life-long dream of owning your own business—entrepreneurship may be the ticket to the future you desire. In this book you'll learn how to pursue this desire without taking undue risks. You'll also take steps to ensure that the business you start is a good fit for you and the marketplace.

Acording to a study reported in the article "Entrepreneurship Remains Strong in 2008 with Increasing Business Startups" by the Ewing Marion Kauffman Foundation, adults ages 55 to 64 are the group most likely to start new businesses; that's us—Baby Boomers! And those slightly younger are not far behind. Yet, as with any large group, Boomers vary significantly in their life situations, needs and reasons for starting businesses.

There are Boomers:
- Planning for retirement and considering starting their own businesses instead of totally quitting work.
- Who are retired but because of financial need, boredom, or any number of reasons, are considering working again, yet they don't want to work for someone else.
- Looking for an alternative to finding a job after having lost theirs because of downsizing, right sizing or a plain old layoff.
- Who always wanted to have their own business and are finally in a position to be able to do so.
- Looking for a way to supplement current or retirement incomes.

In which of the above groups do you fall?

Even though these groups, on the surface, may appear very different, as Baby Boomers starting businesses they have similar needs and concerns. All are likely concerned about protecting the nest eggs they have accumulated as they move forward with their entrepreneurial plans. They are also dealing with the same issues of energy and health that come with age. However, those displaced from a job likely have greater financial urgency to generate an income, as they have not had years to plan for the time when they would leave their jobs behind. Preparation may have been a matter of days or weeks.

Regardless of the situation that brought you to this point in your life, by reading this book and working through the activities included, you are laying a strong foundation for successfully starting your own business.

"Life isn't about waiting for the storm to pass.
It's about learning to dance in the rain."
Vivian Greene

What You Will Take Away

In *BoomerPreneurs* you will answer key questions such as

- What factors should those over the age of 50 consider when starting their own businesses?
- Is starting your own business the right thing for you?
- How do you come up with an idea for a business or, if you have one, know that it fits you and the marketplace?
- How do you evaluate the feasibility and viability of your business idea?
- What research should you do and what type of business plan should you write?
- What steps do you take to start your business?

Over three decades of working with entrepreneurs led me to the realization that more time and effort spent at this early planning stage of the entrepreneurial process reaps tremendous rewards down the road in terms of time and money saved, entrepreneurial satisfaction and success.

My Story

Over the years, as a professor of entrepreneurship and entrepreneurship curriculum consultant, I have worked with hundreds of individuals to help them pursue their entrepreneurial dreams. As an entrepreneur myself, I have also experienced the challenges of entrepreneurship first hand.

I couldn't have retired from my job as a professor of entrepreneurship if I had not already had my own business, which I started on a part-time basis about 10 years prior to retiring. Having my own business allowed me to leave full-time employment at age 55, still generate income and have challenging, interesting work. It provided some of the savings that I accumulated to use in retirement and paid for my daughters' college educations.

I have observed many of my Baby Boomer friends, colleagues and family members wrestle with the question of whether or not to retire or to seek employment after losing a job. A number of them ended up starting their own businesses as an alternative to quitting work totally or returning to the corporate world. Although there is a lot written about how to start businesses, there is little available that addresses the unique needs and concerns of Baby Boomers doing so, starting a business at 50-plus years of age.

This is the market for which this book is written. I know it on a personal level as a Baby Boomer myself and as an entrepreneur who has been involved in a number of ventures over the years, including a limited liability real estate company, small manufacturing company and consulting firm. You'll see references to these entrepreneurial experiences throughout the book.

How This Book Is Organized

In this book you will follow these four steps to business start-up:

- Step 1 What Should Baby Boomers Consider Before Starting a Business?
- Step 2 Recognize the Opportunity That's Right for You and the Marketplace
- Step 3 Refine Your Idea and Do Your Research
- Step 4 Determine Business Viability and Get Started

Steps 1 and 2 address what to do—what type of business to start—focusing first on Baby Boomers, in general, and then on you, in particular. This attention to your specific needs and desires is the important piece I find missing in most books on entrepreneurship.

Step 3. Refine Your Idea and Do Your Research directs you to learn from marketplace winners by identifying Critical Success Factors and provides hands-on research techniques that enable you to obtain answers about product features and benefits and potential market demand.

Step 4. Determine Business Viability and Get Started prompts you to evaluate your business for feasibility from a technical, personal, marketing, management and financial point of view. You also prepare an Abbreviated Business Plan.

Throughout the book, you will find *Action Steps* that allow you to start the work needed to build your business. As with many worthwhile endeavors in life, more is better; the more effort and time you put into completing action steps, the more you will get out of the book.

"There are only two kinds of businesses, small businesses and formerly small businesses."
Author Unknown

Other elements of the book include *Featured Entrepreneurs* at the end of each chapter. Featured Entrepreneurs are Baby Boomers, like you, who started their businesses later in life. Early on, I planned to feature entrepreneurial superstars like those frequently highlighted in the media, but as I progressed in writing this book, it seemed to make more sense to feature Baby Boomer entrepreneurs with stories similar to those of the majority of entrepreneurs I have worked with over the years. These entrepreneurs modeled the behaviors and attitudes discussed throughout the book and exemplified the idea that having your own business is an achievable goal, not an unrealistic dream. Some of these entrepreneurs may end up being superstars; but, for the most part, they are typical entrepreneurs with super stories, which are shared through short vignettes or in one- to two-page excerpts at the end of each chapter.

Research data to support various points are included throughout the book, and practical tips and advice are featured in *Insight or Common Sense.* A word of caution: As with any decisions you make, prior to acting upon any and all information and recommendations included by featured entrepreneurs, experts and this book's author, **perform your own research and consult with the appropriate experts.**

That's a brief look at the path you will follow in the upcoming pages. Let's begin Chapter 1 by taking a closer look at some of the basic decisions 50-plus year olds need to make regarding work.

STEP 1

What Should Baby Boomers Consider Before Starting a Business?

CHAPTER 1

Return, Retire or Reinvent

You, like me and millions of other Baby Boomers, have either reached or are quickly approaching that magical age of 55, the minimum retirement age in many companies. Even if you are not seriously considering retirement right away, this is an age that causes you to consider how much of your time you want to spend working in the next third of your life—for someone else, for yourself, or not at all.

The good news is that Baby Boomers have options. They are educated, youthful in their mental outlook and in relatively good health—"healthy, wealthy, and wise," as one entrepreneur put it. They are looking to their future with anticipation, excitement, anxiety or fear, or maybe they are only afraid of their spouse's retirement! But as you consider retirement,* either because of your age or the loss of a job, from somewhere in the deep recesses of your mind two questions keep tugging at you: "Will I have enough money?" and "If I retire, what will I do?"

If you planned your retirement for years, you probably have a clear idea of what you want in your future, although economic

> *Technically "retirement" refers to when a person quits "producing" but continues consuming. We use the term "retirement" in this book to mean leaving full-time career employment working for someone else. Using this definition, many "retired" workers continue to work (produce) for years.

changes may have caused you to alter the timeframe. If you were asked to retire early or were laid off from your job, you have had much less time to plan and likely feel you are doing so at warp speed. You may find that you need to work for several more years; some feel they will never be able to retire.

Regardless of how you arrived at this point—displacement, pending or current retirement—now you have an opportunity to decide what you want your life to be from here on out, as you ask yourself, "What now?" In the next section, we'll explore your options in more depth.

Return, Retire, Reinvent—Which Is It?

Many factors influence your decision on what to do at this pivotal point. Key questions to ask yourself include

- Will you return to work, and, if so, will you do so for yourself or for someone else?
- Regardless of whether you are working for yourself or others, do you want to work full or part time?
- What type of work do you want to do—something similar to what you've done in the past or something totally different?
- What are your financial goals/requirements for generating an income?

Now let's examine some key factors that will determine how you answer these questions.

Social Security and Insurance

Two very basic issues that likely influence your decision about work are Social Security and health insurance. The following chart identifies the retirement age for receiving full Social Security benefits.

Age to Receive Full Social Security Benefits

*Table found at www.socialsecurity.gov

Year of birth	Full retirement age
1942	65 and 10 months
1943-1954	66
1955	66 and 2 months
1956	66 and 4 months
1957	66 and 6 months
1958	66 and 8 months
1959	66 and 10 months
1960 and later	67

You may opt to receive Social Security benefits as early as 62 years of age, but doing so will permanently reduce your benefits. For example, if you retire at age 62, your benefit would be about 25-30 percent lower than what it would be if you waited to receive it at your full retirement age. In general, the longer you delay taking Social Security, the higher your Social Security benefit.

If you work after becoming eligible for early Social Security, your anticipated earnings is likely the deciding factor in whether or not to take Social Security. If a person takes Social Security early, at age 62, and continues to work and receive wages, there is roughly a one dollar penalty for every two dollars of earned income over $14,160 (2009). If you file taxes jointly with your spouse or even if you are married filing individually, you may be taxed on Social Security benefits if your combined incomes are above certain thresholds. **Be sure to check with the Social Security office for specifics and the most recent rulings regarding age and income.**

Another key consideration is insurance. Baby Boomers who

retire before age 65 (when they become eligible for Medicare) and do not carry health insurance into retirement (this is becoming the norm) are often surprised to learn how hard it is to get insurance and how expensive it is, especially if they have always had access through their employer or spouse. I saw this myself when a family member's health insurance cost in excess of $10,000 a year upon his retiring from work at age 60. At age 65, he will qualify for Medicare; in the meantime, he has five years to fill in the gap.

Insurance is something to research carefully prior to making your decision to leave a job which provides it. It has caused many early retirees to take jobs just for the health insurance benefits.

After carefully considering Social Security and health insurance issues and their impact on your work situation, the next thing to think about is how much time in your future you want or need to spend working.

Leisure-Work Balance

Retirement isn't what it used to be. Or maybe it is, once we understand that for most of human history there has been no such thing as "retirement." When society was mainly one of hunting, gathering and farming, retirement, as we know it today, was not a part of the normal life-cycle. People worked their entire lives.

In more recent decades, retirement has often been triggered by age, influenced by eligibility for Social Security benefits and employers' retirement programs. The stereotyped retirement included retirees heading to the golf course and/or moving to Florida.

For many today, retirement looks very different, as the economy, life expectancies and good health have changed the way many experience retirement. I'm retired, but I work anywhere from 20 to 50 hours a week, and I like it that way.

When asked what they want to do in retirement, many people initially respond they want to spend time enjoying hobbies, traveling, volunteering and visiting family. In other words, they don't want to be tied down to a job in any fashion.

Often later, upon realizing the importance of work in their lives or the realities of their financial situations, they change their minds and start considering working, either part time or full time, as an option. For those who lost a job through job displacement or forced early retirement, retirement may not be a viable option because of the abruptness of their situations.

Whatever your circumstances, clarifying the balance you want between leisure and work is a helpful planning starting point, and you will do so in Action Step 1.1 Leisure-Work Balance. When I completed this Action Step, I realized that I was still very interested in working, at least for the next five to eight years. Yet I wanted to be able to determine my work schedule, which allowed me the flexibility to travel and visit family. On the first Leisure-Work Continuum, I placed my "X" close to "Work." In each of the subsequent ones, my "X" moved to the left, toward more leisure time.

In reflecting on how I would make this transition to less work and more leisure activities, I decided I needed to start identifying and nurturing more hobbies and interests, or ten years from now I would still be working most of the time.

Now it's your turn. Take a moment to determine how you want to divide your time between leisure and work in both the near and the distant future. What do you want the balance to be—now? In the next five years? The next 6-10 years? Eleven or more years from now?

1.1 ACTION STEP
leisure-work balance

On the leisure-work continuum below, "leisure" represents spending all your time devoted to areas of personal interests and fulfillment with no earned income; "work" indicates working approximately 40-plus hours a week, for yourself or someone else, with leisure activities restricted to evenings and weekends. Points in between reflect varying combinations of the two.

On the first continuum, place an "X" indicating the balance of work and leisure you have now. If you are working full time, the "X" will be all the way to the right. On the second, third and fourth, place an "X" indicating the balance of work and leisure you would like to have within the next five years, 6-10 years and 11 or more years. Then answer the question that follows.

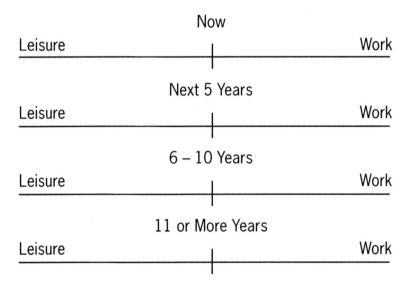

a. What changes need to occur to move from where you are on the "Now" continuum to where you would like to be on the "Next

5 Years" continuum?

b. What changes need to occur to move from where you are on the "Next 5 Years" continuum to where you would like to be on the "6–10 Years" continuum?

1.1

c. What changes, if any, need to occur to move from where you are on the "6–10 Years" continuum to the "11 or More Years" continuum?

In looking at the leisure-work activity you just completed, you probably noticed that the balance between work and leisure changes with age, typically shifting toward more leisure time, for any number of reasons (i.e., health, energy level, fewer work opportunities).

As I mentioned, I currently work anywhere from 20 to 50-plus hours a week. I think I have the best of both worlds—work *and* leisure. I am able to stay involved in my profession, yet most weeks I have time for friends, family and hobbies. But for those weeks when I work about 50 hours or more, the difference between now and my younger years is that I can no longer keep up the pace for too many weeks in a row.

Over the next 5–10 years and beyond, the amount of time I work will decrease. This is partly because my husband is six years older than I am and retired about a year ago. We would like to spend more time traveling and visiting family. It is also because some days I just get tired.

You may be too young to identify with the issue of "getting tired" more easily now than in the past, but, trust me, you will. I don't speak just for myself, but also for my many friends in their 60s.

Now let's look at another factor that influences whether or

not you will likely continue working—the role work plays in your life from an emotional standpoint.

Attachment to Work

Do you really like the work you do? Do you identify strongly with your job? If the answer to both of these questions is "yes," likely you will work in retirement or after being displaced from work, even if financial need is not the driving force. This is because work is an important part of your life. When we define ourselves by what we "do," leaving a job—either voluntarily or involuntarily—can be threatening to our self esteem.

I define myself to some extent by my work. When I retired, I found I was apprehensive about not working. From the literature on the subject, I saw I was not alone. One such study, by Christine Price at Ohio State University, is highlighted here, "Work and Self-Esteem."

How does *not* working make you feel? If you feel somewhat anxious or apprehensive, as I did, complete the *Pause & Reflect* activity that follows. I have found answering the two questions listed to be very beneficial. Over the years, I have repeated these questions to family and friends so frequently that I frequently hear these questions repeated back to me when I am stressed about a particular situation.

By asking myself the first question, I found that the source of my anxiety about

Work and Self-Esteem. A study by Christine Price at Ohio State University reports that "[w]omen doctors, teachers and other professionals may have a tougher time adjusting to retirement than do women who hold jobs customarily considered nonprofessional, such as clerical positions and cafeteria help. They talked about losing their professional identities and, subsequently, feeling a reduction in their social status. In contrast, most women in the nonprofessional group said they were relieved to leave their jobs."

In Price's study of nearly 30 retired women–half of whom had held professional jobs prior to their retirement while the other half had held nonprofessional jobs–she found that "[w]omen in the nonprofessional group explored new interests with no feelings of loss. In comparison, women in the professional group enjoyed the retirement experience overall, yet still felt a sense of loss."

Ohio State Research News Web site at http://researchnews.osu.edu/archive/womret.htm

retirement was threefold; I had a fear that (a) I had not saved enough money, (b) I would be bored and (c) without working, or "producing," I would feel less valuable as a person. Obviously, I had a lot of fears.

Asking myself the second question helped me identify different courses of action to take if these events occurred. My fear of not having enough saved was likely irrational, as I had carefully planned for retirement. My fear of becoming bored was not based on reality as I have always been a person who can think of 99 things to do with my time.

The third concern, regarding my self-value, was a little more challenging. Even though I know it is irrational, I still equate value to productivity: what I do and what I achieve. I define achievement in terms of work.

Taking time to think about what activities, other than work, would give me a sense of achievement and accomplishment has been helpful. New areas I've identified include the following: Health and fitness—working out at the gym four times a week, a more disciplined approach than I currently have; Helping others—starting the volunteer work with a local charity I've been talking about doing for years; and Personal interest—researching interesting and picturesque places to hike and scheduling at least one hike in the next year. When I thought about it, there are many interesting and worthwhile things to do, other than work, that provide a sense of satisfaction and accomplishment.

Coming up with a plan to deal with any anxieties you may have about job loss or retirement is an empowering step; try it yourself.

Financial Requisites

Throughout our lives we have been programmed that certain

Pause & Reflect
Concerning job loss or retirement, what is the worst thing that can possibly happen?

_____

_____

_____

_____

_____

_____

If it happens, how will you deal with it?

_____

_____

_____

_____

_____

_____

milestones are determined by age. At 16 years old, for example, we obtain our driver's license; at 21 years old, we can legally drink. Now at 62 or 65, we retire, right? Not necessarily!

Retirement is a function of assets, not age, which may be a change in mindset for some people. That said, some people retire at 45 years old and some at 75.

As you consider retiring, the big question becomes how much you need in the way of assets to retire. How much money is "enough"? What's the magic number? What you find is that "the number" depends on so many things that it's challenging to determine, and it's different for everyone. There is even a book out titled *The Number*, by Leo Eisenberg, which deals with the subject.

A frequently repeated guide for how much money you will need in retirement is 70–80 percent of your pre-retirement earnings each year. This number, however, appears to assume that you spend most or all of your pre-retirement earnings. Obviously, some people live way below their means, so for them this number is an overstatement of what they need to retire. Others live way beyond their means, and for them this number is not adequate to cover future expenses as their working income is not adequate to cover current expenses.

Financial planning tools are available to tell you "the number." I have used a handy little software program by T. Rowe Price for years. A friend of mine, who has spent hours using the same program, regularly updates me on how long she can live, based on when her money is projected to run out. Her original projection showed she was fine until age 94. More recently with the volatility in the economy, she called to tell me that she can now live only to 86 years of age. We laugh at it at this point in our lives.

Likely your financial planner, if you have one, has shown you charts that indicate when and if your money runs out. You don't want to see red on your charts. Working, either for yourself or someone else, is a way to forestall drawing off those retirement assets until a later time, thus decreasing the likelihood that you will run out of money.

If you have been displaced from your job, you have not had the luxury of planning for this event years in advance. It may be apparent that you need to continue to work to pay the bills. A simple budget or cash flow projection is enough to tell you this. Your decision is not whether to work or not to work, but rather whether to do so for yourself or someone else.

Although financial requirements alone determine how much and how long many people need to work, leisure-work preference and attachment to work will be the determining factors for others.

Work and Baby Boomers

The concept that a person abruptly leaves work at some predetermined age, never to return again, is an antiquated perception of retirement not supported by current research, such as that reported by CBS News correspondent Nancy Cordes. She states that nearly 80 percent of Baby Boomers say they'll work on a part-time basis after their retirement, which is planned for age 63 on the average. The 2008 landmark cross-generational study, *Rethinking Retirement* by Charles Schwab and Age Wave, places that number around 70 percent—that means seven out of 10 pre-retirees plan to work after retirement.

In "Rethinking Retirement," most respondents stated that they prefer working part time rather than full time in retirement, and 60 percent said they would like to work in fields totally different from their current ones. That means many Boomers plan to try new things, and starting their own business may well be one of them.

The Self-Employment Option

If 70 to 80 percent of pre-retirees plan to work after they retire, and you may very well be one of them, ask yourself this question, "Would you rather work for yourself or for someone else?"

According to a 2005 retirement study by Merrill Lynch, 11 percent of the 5,111 Baby Boomers surveyed said that starting their own business was the ideal plan for post-retirement. You'll find similar information in magazines and by browsing the Internet, such as the posting "More Retirees Opting to Launch Startups, Baby Boomers Aren't Just Heading to the Links" at CNNMoney.com

And age isn't the barrier some people think it is. Research by AARP reports that one out of three self-employed Boomers made the leap to self-employment after age 50, either as a transition to retirement or to supplement their incomes and do something they wanted to do.

Self-employment gives Baby Boomers the opportunity to be their own boss, providing the flexibility that many seek. Even working 20 hours a week for someone else may prevent you from doing the things you want to do when you want to do them. Often you are asked to work the "wrong" 20 hours—weekends or evenings—or year round.

Is Now a Good Time to Start a Business?

Well, it depends on what type of business you want to start. But in general, for the types of businesses Baby Boomers start, the answer is "yes." Here are some reasons why:

- Many Boomers are looking to start businesses that have low start-up costs. At 50-plus years old, they want to minimize their start-up investment and the financial risks associated with starting a business. Many self-finance their businesses. As such, tight credit in the current economy will not have the same impact on them as it will on business start-ups that require a lot of capital.
- Opportunities are created by changes in the marketplace, which is definitely something we've seen the last several years. Disruptions in the status quo create opportunities for the alert entrepreneur. One only has to look to history to see examples of companies that have started and flourished in down economies, including General Electric, McDonald's and Microsoft. According to the recent study published by the Ewing Marion Kaufman Foundation, "The Economic Future Just Happened," more than half of the companies on the 2009 Fortune 500 list were launched during a recession or bear market, along with nearly half of the firms on the 2008 *Inc.* list of America's fastest-growing companies.
- Starting a business takes time. If you've just retired or lost your job, time might be the resource you have in great abundance. By using your time to plan, research, develop and test the market, you will be poised to take advantage of economic growth as it occurs. Starting a business in a slower economy provides time for you to learn valuable lessons, gather information and establish a track record that will prepare your business for future growth.
- Many business costs will be lower than in a thriving economy. This can be anything from employee costs (talented employees may find themselves out of work and willing to work for less), rent, office equipment and furniture,

advertising and the like.

- Customers are different. Loyalty to current vendors often loosens in changing markets as buyers look for better value and less expensive product and service alternatives.
- Your opportunity cost may be low. The opportunity cost of a decision is what is given up when you choose one alternative over your next-best alternative. For those who are retired or displaced from their job, the opportunity cost, what they give up by starting their own business, may be their golf hobby or watching *Oprah*.

> *"Twenty years from now you will be more disappointed by the things that you didn't do than by the ones you did do. So throw off the bowlines. Sail away from the safe harbor. Catch the trade winds in your sails. Explore. Dream. Discover."*
> Mark Twain

Here, and at the end of each chapter in this book, a boomer-preneur is featured who exemplifies many of the points included in the chapter. Read how each transitioned from employee to entrepreneur and benefit from their lessons learned along the way.

Introduction to Featured Entrepreneurs

Read in the following entrepreneurial vignette how Bill VanDe-Berghe put his technical background to good use in retirement by starting an Internet-based marketing company along with wife, Vickie. With a goal of adding income to their retirement revenue stream, they grew their business to span all 50 states and 10 foreign countries, their biggest customer being in Australia.

Featured Entrepreneurs Bill and Vicki VanDeBerghe

Fox Hill Farm (FHF) Leather
Retail and wholesale online motorcycle leather
riding apparel, helmets and accessories

Bill VanDeBerghe's financial planner suggested that earning some income during the first 5–7 years of his retirement, after working 30 years at Southwestern Bell Telephone Company, would ensure a secure financial future. An opportunity to do so arose when a friend called Bill to see if he and his wife, Vicki, would be interested in helping him sell merchandise to bike rally vendors at places

Vicki and Bill VanDeBerghe

like Sturgis, Daytona and Myrtle Beach. With that, Fox Hill Farm Leather was launched in spring of 2003.

After traveling to rallies for several months, Bill and Vicki returned home saying, "Here's an opportunity to take what we learned and put the products online to sell over the Internet." Fox Hill Farm (FHF) Leather's retail Web site, www.foxhillfarmleather.com, was launched in December 2003. The product line includes almost everything a motorcycle rider could want—leather riding apparel, sunglasses, helmets and the like.

"We saw an opportunity to use the skills we learned in previous careers to build an Internet business," said Bill. His entire career was spent in the technical side of business and Vicki did photographic work for antiques they sold on eBay. Thus, E-commerce was a perfect fit.

Bill reported that quite a bit of research went into launching their Web site. He found the magazine Practical E-commerce, geared toward businesses with less than a million dollars in sales a year, particularly helpful. Bill and Vicki manage and maintain the Web sites themselves, which significantly reduces expenses and gives them total creative control.

The VanDeBerghes quickly realized that marketing was their biggest challenge. Early on, they learned how to advertise through Yahoo's and Google's Pay-Per-Click to drive targeted traffic to their websites. Additionally, they learned the importance of search engine optimization to improve their positioning in the organic area of search engine results. This enabled them to reduce the amount of expense associated with Pay-Per-Click advertising.

After being up and running for about 18 months, the VanDeBerghes started receiving calls and e-mails from small retailers and rally vendors asking if they could buy wholesale. They liked the diversity of FHF's product line and wanted to be able to purchase products direct. Shortly thereafter, the VanDerBerghes launched their wholesale division as a separate Web site, www.foxhillfarmwholesale.com. Since the summer of 2005, they have acquired more than 1,900 wholesale clients.

"Our marketing efforts this year included some print advertising in industry-specific magazines to reach more wholesale clients. Although it's expensive, we experienced a 30-percent increase in our monthly new accounts after the first month's advertising," said Bill. In the last couple of years, FHF also began publishing print catalogs.

"We got our start on the retail side by purchasing from companies that had no, or very small, minimums," said Bill. We adopted that philosophy for our wholesale business as well." By not setting a minimum purchase, FHF is able to service small accounts that are not served by larger suppliers. FHF's one-stop shopping site for small retailers works well, and wholesale business makes up 85 percent of sales.

Bill reported that the business was totally self-financed, starting with an investment of a couple of thousand dollars. He feels that the financial security his retirement from the phone company provides allowed him to make different decisions than if his livelihood depended on the business. For example, during the first couple of years, all monies were plowed back into the company to finance growth.

Bill and Vicki anticipate receiving their reward at the end when they sell the business.

They will consider doing so when revenues reach $1,000,000. A couple of potential buyers have already approached them. One is a business owner who is looking for an opportunity to buy an Internet-based business that balances his calendar. His busiest seasons are fall and winter. Fox Hill Farm's is spring and summer.

Bill strongly advocates marketing through the Internet. He said, "Look at how people bought 100 years ago—through catalogs. People are very comfortable buying based on a picture of an item."

Bill and Vicki work approximately 25 hours each a week, employing one to two part-time workers as needed. When asked what he would like to share with other Baby Boomers interested in starting their own businesses, Bill said, "The opportunities are endless. Find something you enjoy doing, your personal interest. Then do your research."

Step 1 What Should Baby Boomers Consider Before Starting a Business?

Step 2 Recognize the Opportunity That's Right for You and the Marketplace

Step 3 Refine Your Idea and Do Your Research

Step 4 Determine Business Viability and Get Started

CHAPTER 2

Boomers' Health, Self and Wealth

As Baby Boomers, we have been traveling new paths and redefining aging, careers, and family structure our whole life. This isn't going to change as we carve out new roles in our later years and the way life is lived in our 50s and beyond.

Realizing that we have a reasonable chance of living well into our 90s, many of us are using our wealth of management, financial and marketing experience to start rewarding and fulfilling businesses of our own. We are changing the way retirement is viewed and lived for many reasons, including good health, personal wealth and a positive self-concept.

Boomer Health

Like a lot of my generation, I thought I could stave off the ravages of time by sheer will power if not by eating my blueberries and riding hundreds or thousands of miles on my stationary bike. But despite all those health club memberships, a comment frequently heard from my Boomer friends starts out with, "I remember when I used to be able to . . ." The ending varies: "run five miles," "wallpaper a room in one day," "wash two cars and mow the yard on a Saturday" or "work 16 hours and get up and do it again the next day." Although anecdotal, such comments send the message that things aren't what they used to be. A quick glance in the mirror confirms it, as well.

The good news is, I think, that regardless of the shape we are in, American Boomers can look forward to an unprecedented life expectancy of a record high of 77.9 years, according to 2009 data from the Centers for Disease Control and Prevention. As stated in the best-selling book *Younger Next Year for Women* by Chris Crowley and Dr. Henry Lodge, "Many of us subconsciously assume we will get-old-and-die. In fact, we will probably get-old-and-live. You may live into your 90's, *whether you like it or not.*"

We can thank medical science for most of this improvement in longevity as data are slowly entering public awareness that contradict the stereotype of healthy and health-conscious 55-plus year olds watching their cholesterol and carbs and working out regularly at the gym. According to *Washington Post* staff writer Rob Stein's article, "Baby Boomers Appear to Be Less Healthy Than Parents," "a growing body of evidence suggests that they (Baby Boomers) may be the first generation to enter their golden years in worse health than their parents." I don't know about you, but this scares me.

One of the main contributing factors is that we are a generation that is less physically active than our parents and grandparents were, with daily lives spent sitting behind computers and the steering wheels of automobiles. Thank goodness medical science will save us from ourselves, to some extent. Yet the sheer number of Baby Boomers moving through the health care system is frightening and deemed the perfect storm by many health care professionals.

> *"The only way to keep your health is to eat what you don't want, drink what you don't like, and do what you'd rather not."*
> Mark Twain

Health's Impact on Business Selection

Personal health and energy level is a critical consideration when evaluating potential businesses to start. As my financial planner recently commented to me, "Now is the time to capitalize on our intellectual capital rather than physical capital." His comment was in response to our conversation about Baby Boomers starting businesses. He went on to say that with 20 and 30 years of work experience, Baby Boomers should choose businesses in which their tremendous store of intellectual capital can be tapped rather than ones that require more physical stamina and activity.

You should consider how "senior friendly" businesses are. Online, home based, and many types of service businesses provide the flexibility and working conditions that many 50-plus year olds seek.

You will likely want to avoid those that require long hours, physical labor, standing on your feet most of the time or frequent and extensive travel. Even though these things might not sound bad now, what about five or ten years down the road?

Working in partnership with others is one strategy for being able to manage the workload of your own business while, at the same time, acknowledging your lack of ability or interest in working the 60-plus hours a week that is required in many start-up business situations. My experience with Baby Boomer entrepreneurs indicates that partnerships are more common in this age group than with younger entrepreneurs.

Partnerships can be especially important in retail businesses where long hours, seven days a week, are the norm. You will see many examples of such partnerships throughout this book.

Self-Concept

Years of work experiences and a track record of success result in many 50-plus year olds having a positive self-concept and confidence in their abilities. The same confidence and self-esteem that are assets at the peak of their careers can pose challenges for Boomers when they find themselves working in unfamiliar settings and/or for others who don't value their experience and expertise. Such frustrations serve as a motivator for some to start their own businesses. As one entrepreneur told me, "After a long and successful career, I found myself in a job where I was mentally quitting every day when my every decision was scrutinized or countermanded."

For those who retired at the peak of their careers, retirement can be a threat to self-concept as they lose important anchors in their lives–work, relationships and outer vestiges of who they are, such as office, company vehicle, administrative support and job title. For example, they feel somewhat demeaned when asked the proverbial question upon meeting someone new, "What do you do?" Responding "I'm retired" is often not as gratifying as what they would have responded prior to retirement, such as, "I'm the vice president of marketing" or "I'm a nurse."

Many retirees, experiencing this loss of identity, return to work in some capacity. I wouldn't be writing this book if I hadn't experienced some of these feelings myself.

Boomer Wealth

On the plus side, along with age comes the likelihood of having accumulated resources (savings, investments, real estate) and greater access to capital (loans, investors). Having an adequate financial base is an important factor in being able to work for yourself, a luxury you may not have had in your younger years. And most of us are in a better position financially to start a business than most 20-year-olds. Ask yourself, "Who has more money–my kids or me?"

Nevertheless, BoomerPreneurs should be VERY cautious about risking their retirement nest egg—tapping their 401(k)s and other retirement accounts. A lot depends on how large a nest egg you have and how much of it is required to cover your basic retirement needs. It may be difficult to replace dollars invested in your business that were earmarked for retirement; and you have fewer years to do so prior to the time you may actually need those dollars. Read "Loss of Retirement Funds," which left one entrepreneur unable to have the retirement she had planned.

Even if all goes well, how many years will you operate your business and reap the rewards of a successful venture? And the abysmal failure rates for start-up businesses are enough to scare many people. An often quoted statistic is that half of business start-ups fail in the first four years.

Most definitions of business failure include some reference to the business's lack of financial performance. My definition of business failure is slightly different. It is "a business that fails to meet the founder's goals." Using this definition, many businesses that generate little or no money may be a success if the founder's goals are to give back to the community, have something interesting to do or fulfill a life-long dream.

Loss of Retirement Funds. "Readers need to know being smart and working hard can still lead to failure," said Carol.* She and her husband learned this lesson the hard way after they invested in a retail franchise. "Like many people, we thought if you bought a franchise, you wouldn't fail," she said. "I thought I did my due diligence, but in looking back, I didn't really know what questions to ask." Consulting experts on the financial statements led to mixed advice. One CPA suggested the statements looked "funny," but an attorney and another CPA said they were fine.

"Even if the financial statements the franchisor** provided had been accurate, which they weren't, we would still have failed as even with sales of $750,000 one year, which was high for our type of retail store, we couldn't outsell our high costs—rent at the mall, inventory, shipping, breakage." Not taking a salary for the 3½ years they were in business and working from early morning to 10 and 11:00 at night six days a week were not enough to keep the business afloat.

"I would hate to see people in this age bracket do anything that required them to take money out of their retirement savings to start or run a business, unless it is totally money they don't need. As a result of investing retirement funds in our business, we don't travel much anymore; we can't afford it," said Carol.

She reports that their business experience has changed their priorities. Family was always important, but now they spend even more time with family and grandchildren. "That's what is important to us."

  * Carol is not the entrepreneur's actual name.
** The franchisor has since gone out of business.

So even though the numbers related to business failure are intimidating, this doesn't have to stop you from owning your own business. However, you need to be smart about the type of business you start. Many businesses can be started with little financial risk. And there are ways to reduce personal financial risks as well, such as taking in a financial partner or investors.

Introduction To Featured Entrepreneur

The combined talents of Elizabeth Erlandson and partner Ardith Stuertz enabled them to launch and grow Licorice International into a thriving online mail order and retail business.

Featured Entrepreneur Elizabeth Erlandson

Licorice International
Online mail order business and retail store in Lincoln, Nebraska

For Elizabeth Erlandson and Ardith Stuertz, owners of Licorice International, the caveat not to go into business with friends did not hold true. For some time, Elizabeth and Ardith knew they wanted to start a business together. They carefully assessed the skills each brought to the table and prayed for guidance in their choice of business. Their initial joint endeavor was a consulting firm for non-profits that capitalized on their accounting,

Ardith Stuertz and Elizabeth Erlandson

human resources and public relations backgrounds, "building on what we knew," stated Elizabeth. "The secret of their successful partnership is common core values and mutual respect, a must for a successful long-term business relationship," Elizabeth shared.

Their consulting business afforded Elizabeth and Ardith the opportunity to work together as partners, develop new skills and business contacts and find out what they really enjoyed doing. It also brought home the fact that their business's growth was limited by the number of hours they had available to work. "In consulting, you sell your time," Elizabeth stated. Concluding they needed a product to sell, they were inspired by the story, "Acres of Diamonds," included on page 84, to "look in their own backyard" for their "diamond"—a winning product.

Researching what made a product successful, Elizabeth concluded they were looking for "something people wanted that wasn't readily available." Licorice candy fit the bill, as Elizabeth knew from looking for good black licorice for her husband over the years. Her mother-in-law, Anna, found a small mail order business in Long Island, New York, from which she frequently ordered her son's favorites. When Anna moved into a nursing home and stopped supplying these tasty goodies, her son, Doug, shared an old order form with his wife so she could "surprise" him. She did better than that . . . she bought the business (along with her husband and their good friends, Ardith and John).

Since its founding in 2002, several moves have allowed Licorice International to continue to grow to its present retail location of 4,450 square feet in Lincoln's historic Haymarket district. They offer over 160 types of licorice from 13 countries.

In terms of the future, Elizabeth commented that "Both of us want to do philanthropic work so we are waiting to decide if we want to continue to develop the business, grow it to the next level—which would take an infusion of cash and talent—or sell the business. I am not ready for retirement."

You can find more information on Licorice International by visiting their Web site at www.licoriceinternational.com.

CHAPTER 3
Why Do Boomers Start Businesses?

Boomers start their own businesses for a variety of reasons, but the desire to be their own boss is a key motivator for young and old alike. On its Web site for the 50-plus-year olds, the Small Business Administration (SBA) lists the following five reasons why Baby Boomers start businesses:

1. Be your own boss
2. Improve financial position
3. Leverage a career skill
4. Maintain an active lifestyle
5. Fulfill your life's dream

I encourage you to visit the SBA Web site for topics related to starting a business for those over the age of 50. It is: www.sba.gov/50plusentrepreneur/runningbusiness/index.html

In my experience working with entrepreneurs, reasons Boomers give for starting their own businesses are very similar to the ones listed by the SBA, generally fall into the following categories:

- **Long-term dream** – A desire to have their own business and be their own boss that may have been simmering for decades
- **Income stream** – Additional income to supplement what is needed to cover basic living or retirement needs
- **Financial distress** – Necessity brought on by a lack of financial resources and/or changing economic conditions
- **Boredom** – A desire to stay active and do something meaningful
- **Fear** – The threat of losing a job or having a lack of control over their financial future
- **Giveback** – An opportunity to help others

Long-Term Dream

Who among us cannot boast of having their own Kool-Aid® stand, mowing lawns or babysitting as a child or teen? We figured out at a very young age that we could make money by offering a product or service to a willing customer.

I recall years ago when a neighborhood 9-year-old named Christie knocked on my door asking me if I had any scraps of fabric she could have. I could not tell the little cherub "no," so I rummaged through my remnants and gave her what I found. About a week later, she returned with a rag doll she had made with my fabric and asked if I wanted to buy it for my young daughter. I had to admire her entrepreneurial spirit; of course, I bought the doll.

How did we change from being young entrepreneurs, like Christie, to looking to the corporate world as the source of our income? Likely many of us were encouraged to do so by well-intentioned parents, relatives, friends and our education system. Early entrepreneurial dreams may have been abandoned because of personal and family financial needs and the desire for a "secure" future. Now, with fewer responsibilities, you may be in a position to pursue your dreams of yesteryear, as was the case with Terrie Boguski featured in "Long-Term Dream."

For many people, starting your own business is getting back to your entrepreneurial roots. It may involve starting your own remodeling business or consulting firm. It involves seeing yourself as able to generate your own income rather than depending on someone else to do so for you.

> *"Happy are those who dream dreams and*
> *are ready to pay the price to make them come true."*
> Leon Joseph Cardinal Suenens

Income Stream

It's all about income streams. This is especially true in retirement. Having your own business is one more income stream to add to that coming from savings and investments, your pension (if you are lucky enough to have one) and Social Security. The greater the number of income streams, the better.

With the volatility of the U.S. stock market and economy, many Boomers are approaching retirement with a sense of trepidation—the bedrocks of their retirement plans are set in shifting sand. Research by Professor Alicia Munnell, director of the Center for Retirement Research at Boston College, reports that 43 percent of households are in danger of not being able to maintain their living standard once they retire. This risk is projected to grow over time, and it gets worse for those lower down the income scale.

Earning additional income during retirement can help shore up the foundation of your financial future and allow you to enjoy this stage of your life.

Long-Term Dream. Terrie Boguski thought of having her own business off and on for years. Finally, at age 50, with her three children raised and her husband in a secure job, Terrie decided that she could assume the risks of self-employment. Terrie's story is featured on page 136.

Many of us are physically and mentally able to work into our sixties and seventies, but this window of opportunity doesn't last forever. Every now and then we hear of people working even later, as is the case of our centenarian, Waldo McBurney, featured in "106-Year-Old Entrepreneur Dies." For most of us, however, health and energy factors limit our income-producing years much more than for Waldo McBurney. If we pass them up now, we won't necessarily have the option to work and generate income 10 to 20 years down the road.

In addition to considering your window of opportunity for generating income, consider the opportunity costs of not doing so. We briefly looked at opportunity costs in Chapter 1. If you still have the opportunity to earn income, either by working for yourself or someone else, you may decide that the opportunity cost of a round of golf or lunch with friends versus working for $15, $25, $50, $100 or $200+ an hour is too high.

By extending this concept to totally retiring versus working, the opportunity costs of retiring may be something you decide you cannot afford. Even with your financial bases covered, you may want to continue to earn some income in retirement for travel or luxuries you don't want to take out of retirement funds.

Fear

Many Boomers have lost confidence in the security of their jobs and the ability of the workplace to provide jobs for them in the future. They are starting businesses as a way to address their fears and take the reigns to control their economic futures, many starting businesses while still employed. These part-time businesses may eventually grow to point that the entrepreneurs are comfortable quitting their full-time jobs or be continued on a part-time basis as a fall-back plan in case of job loss.

This fear isn't limited to Baby Boomers, as young people today—hearing parents' concerns or experiencing downsizing in the workplace among their peers—are also looking for ways to take control of their future. I recently talked to a young teacher who had started an Internet-based business, which she ran in the evenings, because of her concern about losing her job. Public employment was once thought to be one of the safest careers a person could have, and now even that isn't insulated from poor economic conditions. She told me that she had come up with the idea for her business through conversations with her 52-year-old insurance agent, who had started an Internet business because of *his* job concerns.

Financial Distress

Over 20 years ago, I attended a presentation on financial planning given by James Stowers III, the founder of American Century Investments. A comment he made has stuck with me to this day. To paraphrase what he said, "There is nothing wrong with being old, and there is nothing wrong with being poor; but to be old and poor is a tragedy."

Who would have anticipated the volatility of the stock market in recent years at a time when Boomers were building their retirement portfolios? For those who were retired, belt tightening became the name of the game as they delayed taking money out of devalued accounts.

Even the most meticulously planned retirement nest eggs can prove insufficient because of longer life spans, inflation, catastrophic health care costs and changes in the economy. And those who lost their jobs are thrown into a financial tailspin as they consider their options. As a result, many Boomers plan to shore up their financial futures by working past the traditional retirement age, often as entrepreneurs owning their own businesses.

Boredom

When looking forward to retirement, many individuals view it as an extended vacation rather than the next third of their lives. Often they meticulously plan their financial futures but pay little attention to how they will spend their time. But after the initial post-retirement euphoria of "the long vacation" wears off and they have completed the big "to-do" list, what then?

Some individuals report a sense of boredom, isolation and lack of purpose in retirement. You'll hear them make remarks similar to those made by Dr. James Sheehan, the Featured Entrepreneur on page 108, that "you can't travel all of the time, and you can only play so much golf." They are looking for something to give meaning to their later years. And many contemplating retirement seem concerned about this possibility. *Rethinking Retirement* by Charles Schwab and Age Wave reports, "While seven out of 10 pre-retirees say they want to work in retirement, the top reason for continued work is not the paycheck—it is to stay mentally active."

Some retirees consider taking a full- or part-time job to fill the void. However, many quickly nix that idea when they determine that there aren't many employment situations in which they will have interesting work, good pay and, at the same time, the ability to set their own hours and take time off to vacation and travel when they want. I frequently hear my retired Baby Boomer friends complain of these restrictions when they flirt with the idea of getting a job. That only leaves them one option—

to make their own job rather than looking to someone else to provide it.

Giving Back

In *Rethinking Retirement,* by Charges Schwab and Age Wave, a reported 45 percent of respondents cite a strong interest in giving back to family and community in retirement. This altruistic motivation influences the types of businesses some entrepreneurs start or what they do with the profits from their businesses.

You have only to look around your community to find examples. Kathy Dibben, the Featured Entrepreneur on page 45, is the founder of Absolute Dignity, a boutique that carries swimsuits, lingerie, wigs and prostheses as a way to reach out to breast cancer survivors (Web site www.absolutedignity.com). As a breast cancer survivor herself, Kathy is devoted to meeting the needs of cancer survivors and is known for her philanthropic work to that end.

> *"The best reason to start an organization is to*
> *make meaning – to create a product or service*
> *to make the world a better place."*
> Guy Kawasaki, entrepreneur, investor, author

Many of today's entrepreneurs demonstrate their concern for their community, the environment and future generations by implementing socially responsible and ecologically sustainable practices in their businesses. Their view of a larger context of "stakeholders" (a person, group, organization or system that affects or can be affected by an organization's actions [*Wikipedia,* free on-line encyclopedia]), holds promise as our world confronts pollution, global warming and health problems related to industrial by-products.

Although solving these problems has historically been seen as the venue of government and big business, entrepreneurs like Karel Samsom and Cynthia Foster, featured on page 120, are increasingly making a difference by assuming responsibility themselves. In their Venice Beach Eco Cottages, they used sustainable and non-toxic building materials and solar power, as well as paints and finishes with no/low VOCs (volatile organic compounds [solvents released into the air as the paint dries]).

On a national and global level, entrepreneurs like Bill Gates have changed the nature of philanthropy and taken the lead in charitable giving and leadership on a worldwide scale. An example of philanthropy related to the topic of this book is that of the late Ewing Marion Kauffman, who founded the Kauffman Foundation, the world's largest foundation devoted to entrepreneurship. His entrepreneurial spirit led him to start his own pharmaceutical company in the basement of his home, which he named Marion Laboratories, Inc. When he sold his company to Merrell Dow in 1989, it had grown to become a global, diversified health care giant with nearly $1 billion in sales and employing 3,400 associates. Later in life, he turned his attention to encouraging and supporting the entrepreneurial growth of others through the Kauffman Foundation.

Consider how your business can contribute to your community as well as a healthy environment for your children and grandchildren. And nowadays, doing so is often the source of a competitive advantage in the marketplace.

"I don't know what your destiny will be, but one thing I do know: the only ones among you who will be really happy are those who have sought and found how to serve."
Albert Schweitzer

Now that you have had a chance to consider the most common motivations for starting a business, take a moment to contemplate the source of your own interest in becoming an entrepreneur by completing Action Step 3.1 below.

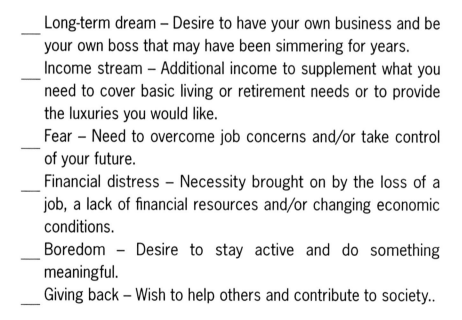

ACTION STEP 3.1
motivation for start-up

Identify the key reasons why you would like to own your own business by placing a checkmark by all answers that apply.

___ Long-term dream – Desire to have your own business and be your own boss that may have been simmering for years.

___ Income stream – Additional income to supplement what you need to cover basic living or retirement needs or to provide the luxuries you would like.

___ Fear – Need to overcome job concerns and/or take control of your future.

___ Financial distress – Necessity brought on by the loss of a job, a lack of financial resources and/or changing economic conditions.

___ Boredom – Desire to stay active and do something meaningful.

___ Giving back – Wish to help others and contribute to society..

In Action Step 3.1, you probably found that you are motivated to start your own business by several factors. I did. My reasons included: (a) Boredom – The desire to stay active and do something meaningful, (b) Income stream – Additional income to supplement retirement, and (c) Long-term dream – A desire to have my own business which had simmered for years. Related to this latter point, I recall telling friends more than two decades ago that being a professor was the closest I could come to being an entrepreneur yet still receive a steady pay check.

Introduction To Featured Entrepreneur

Giving back was the major factor that motivated Kathy Dibben to start a business in which she is able to help other breast cancer survivors find products that fit their needs.

Featured Entrepreneur Kathy Dibben

Absolute Dignity
Retail store specializing in post-breast surgery products,
swimwear, lingerie, wigs and soft headwear

Having your picture on over 20 million cereal boxes is the kind of publicity most entrepreneurs could only dream of. When Kathy Dibben of Absolute Dignity, a retail specialty boutique in Smithville, Missouri, was first contacted about being featured on General Mills cereal boxes, she thought it was a hoax.

Kathy is a two-time breast cancer survivor. General Mills discovered Kathy through her company's Myspace Web site and wanted to include her, along with four other ambassadors for Pinktogether.com, their breast cancer awareness campaign on cereal boxes. Kathy was later also featured on Fiber One Bars and Chex Mix Select.

Kathy Dibben in front of her store

The idea for Kathy's business came from the total frustration she experienced trying to find post-surgery products following breast cancer surgery. The final straw was trying to find a mastectomy swimsuit to wear to her son's wedding in Cancun. After calling everywhere, she finally found a pool equipment and chemical business that had a few swimsuits in the back of the store. Kathy thought, "This isn't right. I'm not the only one going through this." Her intuitive feeling about the need for a place were cancer survivors could find the products they needed in a personal and caring environment was confirmed through frequent conversations with other breast cancer survivors.

With a son attending law school in California, funds were short. This deterred Kathy from seriously considering opening a shop until one day when her husband came home from doing carpentry work on retail space owned by her brother and sister-in-law and announced, "I just built the space for your shop." He encouraged Kathy to tell her brother and sister-in-law that she was interested in the space if their present tenant ever moved out. That opportunity occurred less than six months later, to which Kathy's response was, "I'm not ready." After everyone in the family said, "I'll help you," Kathy revisited the business plan she had started four years earlier with a new resolve. Absolute Dignity opened in June 2007.

In addition to product selection, customers say what sets Absolute Dignity apart from other shops is that they can "feel the warmth and positive energy" when they come in. As a certified specialist in fitting customers with prostheses and wigs, Kathy has a passion for making sure that her products "truly fit right." Her desire to personally work with customers and the difficulty of finding others with similar certifications and compassion have resulted in Kathy regularly working 60-plus hours a week.

A financial background did not preclude Kathy from making some financial decisions that she wished she had not made. She is still challenged by the credit card debt she incurred to purchase the inventory for her business. Kathy felt that credit cards were her only financing option, albeit not a good one, with little start-up capital and no bank financing—a common problem for new businesses. She cautions others to learn from her experience and start out with more working capital.

You can find more information on Absolute Dignity by going to their myspace page at www.myspace.com/absolutedignity or their Web site at www.absolutedignity.com.

CHAPTER 4

What Businesses Are Boomers Starting?

Determining the type of business to start can be a challenging task. Two key determinants are a person's work experience and motivation for starting a business. Let's look at both in greater depth.

Work Experience and Type Of Business

A person's work experience—its breadth, depth and versatility—influences the type of business he or she starts. This isn't the only factor, certainly, but it is one of the most significant. Let's examine major work categories and likely business start-ups.

- **Workers with technical backgrounds**. As you might have guessed, these workers are likely to start businesses related to technology. What I think will surprise you is that contrary to the widely held image of the young whiz kid starting a tech business in the garage, aging Boomers are even more likely to dive into the technology pool, as shown in "Age of Entrepreneurs when Starting

Technology Businesses."

- **Professionals.** Many professionals (i.e., nurses, accountants, and attorneys) stretch their wings by starting businesses offering their skills directly to customers rather than working for others that do. The good news is that these types of businesses are among those having the highest profit margins, according to research by Sageworks, a Raleigh-based financial services software company.

- **Management**. The types of businesses Boomers with managerial backgrounds start vary greatly as they use their managerial skills and strong personal networks to launch businesses that may or may not be related to industries in which they have worked. The broad exposure and skill-mix of management prepares them for the Jack-of-all-trades role of an entrepreneur.

- **Encore careers.** Loosely defined as careers that combine income with social purpose, encore careers appeal to many Boomers. Such careers may be related to previous work or in totally new fields. Strong social networks developed over decades in the workplace are an advantage many bring to these careers.

- **Hobbyists**. Turning a hobby into a business allows some Boomers to make money while doing something they love.

"Small opportunities are often the beginning of great enterprises."
Demosthenes

Motivation and Type of Business

For workers with a long-term desire to own their own business, the industry they choose is often secondary to the opportunity to act entrepreneurially. The businesses they start may be different than the ones in which they have spent their careers, as owning their own business is the primary motivator rather than owning a particular type of business. Such was the case for the founders of Licorice International, our entrepreneurs featured on page 33, who made a concerted search for a product to sell. This led them into a whole new industry, the candy industry.

For many, starting their own business is a more desirable option than returning to the corporate world after being downsized; for some, it is an option of last resort after an unsatisfactory job-seeking experience. Of the 200 customers who responded to an online survey from Ring Central, a toll-free or local hosted phone service for small businesses, approximately 22 percent reported they were downsized from their jobs. Many of these downsized workers choose businesses related to what they know—previous work or hobbies.

A close friend of mine exemplified this approach to entrepreneurship when she was downsized from a large company. Her initial thoughts were to return to work somewhere else. I encouraged her to enroll in the entrepreneurship course that I was teaching for displaced workers through a local outplacement firm. At first, her response was that she had no interest in having her own business. But after months of looking for employment, she came to the realization that self-employment was her best option. Capitalizing on her strong organizational skills, she subcontracted her services to a seminar company and mortgage broker and remains self employed to this day, eight years later.

Some workers see having their own businesses as a way to augment their income from a full-time job. Possibly they would really like to own their own business, but, because of their high security needs, they can't bring themselves to quit their full-time jobs. They start their businesses while still holding a job, working evenings and weekends until they gain the confidence that their new business will support them. These businesses are often related to what they know—their full-time employment or an avid hobby.

Throughout this book, note how Featured Entrepreneurs' work experiences and motivation influenced the types of businesses they started.

Other Considerations

Baby Boomers, particularly as they approach retirement, are interested in starting businesses with low start-up costs and which afford them considerable flexibility in their work schedules. Web-based and some service businesses provide entrepreneurs considerable control over when and where they work, and they provide this with minimal investment.

Insight or Common Sense
Do your due diligence before entering into a franchise agreement or buying an existing business. Verifying the information provided and conducting your own research is the key to making an informed decision.

Entering into a franchise arrangement is a strategy for other Boomers who do not want to start a business from scratch but prefer to have the training and assistance that most franchisors provide. Steve Strauss, author of The Small Business Bible, encourages individuals to consider franchises—businesses in which you pay a fee to gain the right to sell or distribute the product of a larger company. In "7 Tips for Retirement Entrepreneurs" at bankrate.com, Strauss is quoted as saying, "A franchise makes sense if it's a proven franchise with a clear-cut return. Not all franchises are created equal. Talk to other franchisees. Make sure it's legit, that you get a good location and that they have a good system."

Another avenue worth investigating is to buy an existing

business. Doing so may provide many of the same benefits as a franchise—name recognition, established procedures, suppliers, financial data, and so on—without the franchise fee. One key question to determine is why the entrepreneur is selling the business. In addition to asking the seller, talk to customers, vendors, landlords and others in the industry.

Introduction To Featured Entrepreneur

The flexibility to be able to travel extensively was a key motivator in Susan Davidson's decision to start a consulting business. Her travel experiences also strongly contributed to her effectiveness in providing services to foreign managers and their families coming to the United States.

Featured Entrepreneur Susan Davidson

Beyond Borders, Inc.
Leadership training, executive coaching and services to accelerate the integration of foreign managers and their families coming to the U.S.

Susan Davidson launched her business, Beyond Borders, Inc., in April, 2002 to provide

Susan Davidson, Beyond Borders, Inc.

services to help integrate international managers and expatriates and their families into the social and business communities of the United States. Her business quickly grew to include executive coaching and leadership training, as well.

Susan has a passion for the international community. On any given Saturday night, a dinner party at her home might include guests from Russia, France, Germany or Kenya. She has traveled extensively, 28 countries in all, studying Spanish in Guatemala and French in the south of France.

A visit with a Service Core of Retired Executives (SCORE) counselor at the Small Business Administration (SBA) helped Susan develop her business idea into a workable plan. Her SCORE counselor, a retired international marketing executive, advised her that a real need/niche was to work with non-Americans to assist them in the otherwise difficult and frustrating process of adapting and integrating into the U.S. community and workplace. He counseled her that most U.S.-based global companies spend the majority of their relocation funds to help American expatriates make the transition into their foreign assignments—but often ignore the needs of in-bound transferees to the United States.

Following several consultations with her SCORE counselor, Susan conducted an online survey with 63 international professionals, followed by in-depth one- to two-hour telephone interviews with 32 of the respondents to gain a thorough understanding of the challenges and obstacles they had encountered in their efforts to live and work in the United States. Susan used her research findings to write articles and give speeches in the Atlanta area--all in an effort to raise her credibility and visibility as a cross-cultural specialist.

While learning the intercultural field, Susan also spoke with a former corporate colleague who had become a certified executive coach. The colleague encouraged Susan to investigate coach training programs and become a formally trained coach. As a result, Susan enrolled in a program accredited by the International Coach Federation. The 18-month teleclass program prompted her to launch a business coaching career as well. Working with American corporations and several prestigious Fortune 500 companies for 25+ years gave Susan credibility in the corporate world and allowed her to speak knowledgably with her clients.

To build her coaching practice, Susan initially offered complimentary sessions to friends, other new coaches and family members, which gave her the opportunity to practice her coaching skills and build her confidence. She then began charging a small fee ($25) for one-hour coaching sessions, which gradually increased to $150 to $250/hour, the average fee for business coaching. When Susan "went public," she let all of her friends and business contacts know that she was offering coaching services and looking for prospective clients.

The growth of Susan's executive coaching practice was partially the result of the increased understanding and endorsement of executive coaching within the Human Resource community. Many major corporations (and a growing number of U.S. government agencies) are now including executive coaching as a method for developing their executive and high-potential leadership talent.

Susan's business allows her to fulfill her personal and financial goals of having freedom and flexibility in her work while at the same time making a comfortable income. This freedom allows time for travel, both domestically and internationally, and for Susan to have control over her day-to-day work/play schedule.

Susan's advice to other Baby Boomers interested in starting their own business is to:

1. Have a nine-month cash reserve that can sustain you while you develop your business. Assume you will make zero income for up to nine months. In other words, plan for the worst and hope for the best---but you must plan to live on savings or other income for a good part of the year, unless you already have clients when you open your doors.
2. Already have prospective clients lined up and be ready to make sales calls: That is, identify, contact and speak with prospective clients on the telephone or face to face about your services and how they might serve their needs. Building your business is a contact sport!
3. Be visible in building your network and prospective client base. Marketing (i.e., a Web site, brochure, business cards, articles or speeches, etc.) is not enough. Ultimately, you must sell. The selling process begins when you get to the point where you engage in a one-on-one conversation with a prospective client about how your business services might address that client's needs. To do business, you eventually must talk to a person, determine his or her needs and offer a solution (i.e., a detailed discussion, written proposal, or formal presentation).

   For more information, go to www.beyondborders.us.

CHAPTER 5

Caveats for Starting a Business at 50-Plus Years of Age

I've worked with entrepreneurs from 18 to 70 years old. The entrepreneurial planning process is similar, regardless of age; but the 50-plus age group is typically at a very different point than their younger counterparts financially, personally and professionally. Along with these differences come unique concerns that need to be carefully considered and addressed.

Financial Risks—How To Reduce Them

Even though you are likely to have savings and assets to invest in your business or use for collateral, much of the money you have is probably spoken for—to pay for your children's college or your retirement. Parting with any of your money to start your business may be painful. Most start-up situations require more dollars than you anticipate, and the more the business grows, the more money it will need.

When your business succeeds, everyone is happy—you, your family, investors and your banker if you sought outside funds.

But what if the business does not succeed? Then what?

Without a proven track record, most investors must know you personally in order to put their hard-earned dollars in your hands. So if you've raised money by taking in investors, it's likely they are friends and family members, as is common in most start-up situations. If things don't go well with your business, you will have to look at their long faces and accusing eyes every Thanksgiving and Christmas for the rest of your life!

If you are able to attract professional investors and the business struggles or fails, you could lose it to unhappy stockholders if they muster the votes to replace you with someone they feel can lead the business more effectively.

If you borrow money, you have a different problem if your business fails. If you cannot repay your loan, the doors to your business may be closed by the courts. If you use your home as collateral for a loan, you could lose that as well. Even if you decide that you can handle the risks associated with borrowing capital, money may not be that easy to find, especially with the tightening of credit markets. And most loans come with a list of qualifications including equity and collateral requirements.

So both borrowing funds and taking in investors carry risks. But don't give up! Consider the following strategies that enable you to reduce the financial risks of starting your business:

- **Choose a Business with Low Start-Up Costs and Keep Expenses Low.** Avoid businesses that require large investments in inventory and either long leases or building a facility. Many service, home-based and online businesses are relatively inexpensive to start and can be self-financed.

  It also goes without saying that you should minimize operating expenses whenever possible. In-home offices and virtual employees and teams allow entrepreneurs to keep

Insight or Common Sense
Limit your borrowing. (Zero would be nice.) Your chances of succeeding are better without carrying a large debt and interest burden.

overhead and travel costs low.

- **Take in a Partner.** You may want a partner for financial reasons or to work in the business as well.

    My experience indicates that Baby Boomers are more apt to be involved in partnerships than younger entrepreneurs. Perhaps with age, the drive to go it alone diminishes, or maybe we just see the wisdom of not trying to do everything ourselves. Notice that over half of the Featured Entrepreneurs have business partners who contribute financially and/or share the work.

- **Look for Industries with Higher-Than-Average Success Rates.** Some industries have higher success rates than others. Choosing a business in one of these industries increases the odds in your favor from the start. For example, in his posting at www.smallbiztrends.com, Scott A. Shane, professor of entrepreneurial studies at Case Western Reserve University, states, "The data [from Amy Knaup of *Monthly Labor Review*] show that the four-year *survival rate* in the information sector is only 38 percent, but is 55 percent in the education and health services sector. That is, the average start-up in the education and health sector is 50 percent more likely than the average start-up in the information sector to live *(survive)* four years. That's a huge difference."

    In general, companies that sell to other businesses also tend to have a higher survival rate than those that sell directly to consumers. Perhaps this is because the entrepreneurs who start these business have considerable experience and knowledge of the industry.

- **Rethink Your Idea.** Sometimes by even slightly altering your business concept, you can significantly reduce the start-up costs involved. For example, instead of opening a restau-

Combined Skills. Renee and Kelly, sisters-in-law, combined their artistic training and talents and a hobby of making jewelry into a full-time business selling jewelry through a Web site and at local events.

Insight or Common Sense
Look for compatibility in values and goals in choosing a partner.

Pause & Reflect
If you already have a business idea in mind, what steps can you take to minimize the financial risk of the business?

_____

_____

_____

_____

_____

_____

_____

_____

_____

_____

_____

_____

_____

rant, which requires a huge capital investment, would you be happy with a catering business at a fraction of the start-up costs? Instead of having a retail store, what about a kiosk in the mall? Start small, and test the market for your products or services.

- **Start Your Business While Still Working.** By continuing to work, any profits you make can be reinvested to fund your business's growth; and you will be able to pay your bills without relying on your business for income. Working in your business part-time also allows you to test the demand for your product or service.

Having a low financial risk tolerance myself, I have implemented a number of these strategies over the years to reduce my financial exposure. When my daughters were young, I wasn't willing to jeopardize their financial security to pursue my entrepreneurial interests. I only pursued ideas in which I could manage the risks. For example, there were multiple partners in two ventures in which I was involved which spread the financial risks. Now that I'm older, I don't want to jeopardize my retirement. My consulting business was low risk by its very nature, and I started it while still working full time.

Starting a business doesn't have to involve large financial risks; think of steps you can take to eliminate some, or most, of the risks involved and record your thoughts in the *Pause & Reflect*.

The Impact of Your Health On Your Business, and Vice Versa

In his article "7 Tips for Retirement Entrepreneurs," Mark Terry advises retirees to "be realistic about the level of physical and mental energy you are willing or able to pour into your work. Some businesses can be run comfortably from your deck with a laptop computer and a cold beverage at your elbow. Others require significant physical labor—such as owning a bakery, restaurant or bed and breakfast."

Sometimes the physical requirements of a job are not as obvious as with the businesses just mentioned. Factors such as heavy travel and a hectic schedule also take their toll. Travel for personal pleasure is one thing; the pressure of standing in long airport lines and waiting for delayed flights while on a business trip is something entirely different. The money may not be enough to compensate for the stress and aggravation or what you are giving up—a round of golf, lunch with friends or time with grandchildren.

Long hours is another challenge, especially in retail business-es, in which it can be difficult to find good and reliable workers who are willing to work evenings and weekends. Business-to-business sales, rather than business-to-consumer sales, likely provides a much more lifestyle friendly schedule.

Energy and health are among my first considerations when evaluating potential growth opportunities for my business. Even though seminars and workshops are one way to grow sales, they take a lot of energy and often involve travel or working to 9:30 or 10:00 in the evening—been there, done it; too old for it except on a very limited basis!

Taking age and related health factors into account causes many Boomers to opt for "lifestyle businesses," ones that afford entrepreneurs the opportunity to balance the demands of the business with their personal priorities.

Addressing Experience Gaps

Whether you are entering a relatively new field or are new to having your own business, here are some ways you can jump start your learning curve.

Work in the Field

For younger entrepreneurs, I recommend that they work a minimum of two to three years in the field in which they plan to start a business, preferably in an entrepreneurial setting. This is good advice for anyone; but at 50-plus years old, you might like to get started a little more quickly.

Any time you can devote to working in your new field will reap tremendous benefits. Consider working part time, perhaps while you keep your regular job, to gain experience. Any job that gives you exposure to the new industry in which you will be operating, even one you feel is beneath your skill level, can be a learning experience.

Find a Mentor. Yes, Even at This Age

Identifying a mentor can be an important next step on your entrepreneurial journey; most successful entrepreneurs report having one. Some identify a series of mentors who guided them along the way, as their mentoring needs changed as their businesses grew.

Mentors are likely to be other entrepreneurs or professionals who know the ropes of launching and growing a business. They may also be friends or former colleagues who have started their own businesses. Mentoring relationships may grow out of friendships developed through clubs, industry associations or volunteer activities. Like other relationships, they grow slowly and take time and energy on the part of both parties.

Your community may have an entrepreneurial mentoring program, as mine does. These are typically started by very successful local entrepreneurs as a way of "giving back" to their communities. Free online mentoring is also available through SCORE. Their Web site address is: score.org/ask_score.html

Yet another source of mentoring may be a "competitor at a distance." This is someone with a business like yours but outside your trade area. Such persons may be valuable sources of hands-on information, as long as your business does not compete with theirs. These "competitors at a distance" can be located through the *Yellow Pages* from other communities, the Internet, your trade association or by talking with people in the industry.

If you explain that you are starting a similar business but will not be operating in their trade area, such entrepreneurs may be more than willing to help you. An introduction through a third party is even better than approaching them as a "cold call," although I know entrepreneurs who have done so successfully. One was a student who developed a mentoring relationship with an entrepreneur hundreds of miles away; he had identified this person through the *Yellow Pages* for a class assignment in which he was asked to interview a "competitor at a distance." The entrepreneur owned an Internet cafe similar to the one he wanted to start. The mentoring relationship continued for several years.

To be successful, mentoring relationships need to be a win-win. The reward for the mentor is often the feeling of satisfaction that comes from "giving back," helping others.

Personal coaches may fulfill mentoring roles for some entrepreneurs, as was the case with entrepreneur Kathy Yeager, featured here in "Preparation and Coaching Key to Successful Launch."

Insight or Common Sense
It's hard to know what you don't know. Nurture relationships with those who are more knowledgeable and experienced in the field and who can guide you during the early and growth stages of your business.

Preparation and Coaching Key to Successful Launch. After working 30 years in Workforce Development and Continuing Education at Johnson County Community College, Kathy Yeager decided it was time to retire. She started planning her retirement a year in advance, recognizing that other colleges would benefit from her sales and marketing expertise and experience.

That's when Kathy contracted with a personal coach, who worked with her an hour a month on such things as identifying her products and targeting her market. "My coach helped me stay focused on the next steps to start and develop the business. She really helped me find the right resources, focus on my core business and set goals," Kathy said. In addition, Kathy sought the services of the Small Business Development Center at her college where she received guidance on business concept development and the preparation of her business plan. By the time Kathy retired, her consulting business was off to a strong start, with clients from across the country.

Contract Training Edge, LLC, is a resource for colleges nationwide in the area of solution selling, workforce development, benchmarking, reorganization and restructuring, and one-on-one coaching. For more information, contact Kathy Yeager at 913-593-5347, kyeager@ctedge.net, or www.ctedge.net.

Volunteer Your Services

A carefully selected volunteer situation in the right setting can allow you to grow and learn in the area in which you will eventually open your business. You will have the opportunity to contribute and at the same time learn new skills and, possibly, a new industry. While you are learning, you are also expanding your network of people who may be helpful to you down the road. And it's hard for others to turn down "free" labor. Unpaid positions are not strictly for 20-year-old student interns.

Early in my career, I learned a great deal about start-up ventures while volunteering in a small business incubator called the Center for Business Innovation, a place designed to accelerate the growth of entrepreneurial businesses. Later on, two of my business consulting clients came from contacts I made while working at the incubator. Read "Volunteering Leads to Partnership" for another example of how a volunteer situation proved beneficial to all parties involved.

Develop New Skills

The less experience you have in the field, the steeper the learning curve. Plus running a business, especially if it's your first, has its own learning curve. So hang on, you're in for an exciting adventure!

In addition to the technical knowledge of your business (what you will do in your business), you need the following business knowledge:

- Sales and marketing know-how, including advertising, promotion and publicity
- Financial know-how, including bookkeeping, accounting and taxes (or the knowledge to interpret the information provided by your certified public accountant (CPA) or bookkeeper
- Production, purchasing and distribution, if you are selling a product
- Legal issues affecting your business
- Knowledge of employment law— if you have employees

Early on, you have to be somewhat a Jack of all trades and perform many of these functions yourself. Gradually you will be able to expand your team to include others who have these skills. In areas such as taxes and employment law, you'll need expert advice from the beginning.

"Entrepreneurship is a team sport."
Author Unknown

With my consulting business, I started out doing almost everything myself. Luckily my work as an entrepreneurship profes-

Volunteering Leads to Partnership
Delena Stout's business partner volunteered at Brookside Barkery and Bath for over a year prior to their formalizing their partnership arrangement. This gave both partners the opportunity to work together and test their compatibility. See Featured Entrepreneur on page 68.

sor helped prepare me, even though I still hired an attorney for legal advice and a CPA for accounting and tax assistance. Now I have a "virtual team" that includes a half a dozen resources, including a fulfillment company that does my invoicing and college textbook shipments, an accountant who visits quarterly, a tax attorney with whom I consult yearly, a proofreader, editor and graphic artist whom I hire by the project, and a marketing/sales consultant and personal friend whom I pay by buying her lunches at our periodic meetings.

Talking to entrepreneurs and others in the field is an excellent way to identify the resources you need. Contact your local SBDC or SBA office for help identifying resources as well. The SBDC is a cooperative effort of the private sector, the educational community and federal, state and local governments, and provides assistance to current and prospective small business owners. SCORE, "Counselors to America's Small Business," is a nonprofit association and partner with the U.S. Small Business Administration. Their goal is to educate entrepreneurs in starting and growing small businesses nationwide. Both offer free services to entrepreneurs and can be found through their Web sites: SBA:http://www.sba.gov/localresources, SBDC:http://www.sba.gov/aboutsba/sbaprograms/sbdc/index.html

A heads up. You will be heavily involved in the sales and marketing of your products/services, especially early in the business. It falls to you to test market demand and grow your business to the point where you may be able to hire others to assist with these functions. If you are not knowledgeable of sales and marketing, consider enrolling in sales or marketing courses through your local college or sign up for one of the short "how-to" courses offered through your local SBA or SBDC. Talking to entrepreneurs selling similar products or marketing consultants is also helpful. Complete Pause & Reflect here.

Other Steps To Improve The Odds Of Success

A friend of mine, a serial entrepreneur, demonstrated what it takes to succeed as he planned to build a car wash with a couple of business partners. He spent countless hours researching the market—area demographics, the competitive environment, traffic and population density patterns in the area—writing a business plan and lining up financing.

Compare that to another person I knew from my frequent visits to the photocopy center at the college where I worked. One day while waiting for my copies, the photocopy operator, knowing that I taught entrepreneurship, announced he was starting his own business. He went on to say, "A friend and I were having a couple of beers last night, and we decided to start our own print shop. He has some experience in printing also, and we each have a number of credit cards that we thought we would use to finance the business." It was only a few weeks later that he disappeared from the photocopy center to get his business started. In less than six months he was back.

"When you don't know where you're going,
any road will take you there."
Lewis Carroll

Although research, planning, a written business plan (an abbreviated one at least) and adequate financing will not ensure success, it greatly increases the odds of it occurring.

Another factor that often differentiates successful entrepreneurs from others is that they search out niche markets. They

Pause & Reflect
If you already have a business idea in mind, in what areas do you have experience or knowledge gaps and how might they be addressed?

——————————
——————————
——————————
——————————
——————————
——————————
——————————
——————————
——————————
——————————
——————————

have often been able to identify an underserved market whose needs are not being adequately met. This is an effective strategy for those who start businesses in the same field as their former employers. They don't compete head-to-head. They carve out a niche that their former employer has either overlooked or ignored. This is also an effective strategy for competing with large companies. Often they are not successful in serving some of the smaller niche markets.

STEP 1 CONCLUSION: WHAT SHOULD BABY BOOMERS CONSIDER BEFORE STARTING A BUSINESS?

After reading the previous five chapters and completing the various activities, you now have a better understanding of your motivation for starting a business and the role you expect your business to play in your life. You are aware of how your health or energy level may have an impact on the business you start and have considered ways to reduce the financial requirements of doing so. You also have considered various avenues that are available to you to build or strengthen the business and entrepreneurial skills you need.

Now you will capture your thoughts on these key points in Action Step 5.1.

5.1 ACTION STEP
step 1 conclusion, my Boomer considerations

Using the framework of the next five years, answer the questions below.

a. What balance between leisure and work would you like to have over the next five-year time period (i.e., mostly work with leisure activities restricted to evenings and weekends, about a 50-50 mix between leisure and work, mostly leisure activities)?

5.1

_____

_____

b. What is your primary reason for starting a business?

_____

_____

c. What impact, if any, do you expect your health to have on your ability to work and run your own business?

_____

_____

d. What impact, if any, does your financial situation have on your ability to start your own business?

_____

_____

e. If you have a business idea in mind, what steps did you identify to reduce the financial risks of starting the business?

_____

_____

f. If you have a business idea in mind, what steps did you identify to overcome any experience or knowledge gaps that existed?

_____

_____

Introduction To Featured Entrepreneur

Delena Stout turned a negative, losing her job, into a positive, starting a very successful pet nutrition and bath store, that has grown to three locations in just five years. Delena improved her odds of succeeding in this venture by taking the entrepreneurial strategic planning course, FastTrac® NewVenture™ prior to starting her business. FastTrac® programs provide existing and aspiring entrepreneurs with key business insights and skills and are delivered through over 300 alliance organizations throughout the U.S. To locate a FastTrac® program near you, go towww. fasttrac.org.

Featured Entrepreneur Delena Stout

Brookside Barkery and Bath
Pet nutrition and bath stores

As a displaced worker, Delena Stout had strong reservations about returning to the corporate world, in spite of former jobs with great pay, travel on corporate jets and work with boards of directors.

During her career, she had worked in accounting, office management and, most recently, sales and marketing for an architectural firm, but it was through her pets that Delena came up with her idea for a business. "We

Delena Stout (in the middle)

have large dogs. Local places to wash dogs were not clean, had bad equipment, or were inconvenient as large dogs were required to climb up a ladder for a bath," she stated.

By crunching the numbers in the Kauffman Foundation's FastTrac® NewVenture™ program, Delena determined that her business idea—offering self-serve pet baths—would need some fine-tuning to become more profitable. She was able to make the needed adjustments as a result of the information she obtained while researching the market. "During a trip to the library in class, I learned how to get on line and pull up periodicals and newsletters. I delved into layers and layers of research material, and it kept opening doors for me. It was the most fascinating thing I ever did," Delena reported.

"My research on other pet health stores around the country helped me decide to focus on quality," Delena said. Noting that "there wasn't any place in town where we could find good quality pet food," Delena combined pet nutrition with her earlier concept of self-serve baths. Hence her business—Brookside Barkery and Bath—was founded in 2003 with a commitment to the health and wellness of pets, stocking the "best quality natural and holistic pet food in the country."

"Through my research," Delena stated, "I learned I was taking a big risk – I was not doing what everyone else was doing. Because I was the first to start this type of business in the area, initial financing was difficult to obtain. Finally, a local bank gave me a loan of $25,000; my husband and I took out savings to finance the rest."

Customer response confirmed that there was a need for this type of store and two additional locations have been opened in the Kansas City metropolitan area, with plans to franchise the business in the near future, Delena reports.

The business's growth required Delena to work extremely long hours, which she has since partially addressed by taking in a business partner. Delena reports that "it gave me back my sanity." She and her partner worked together for about a year before formalizing a partnership arrangement, making sure it was the right fit for both of them.

"Every job I have had in my entire life prepared me for this," Delena said. "Because of my background in marketing, I knew what avenues to use to market the store. My exposure to accounting enabled me to read the business financial statements. Through various work experiences, I also learned what not to do. I would never treat my employees the way I have seen some people treat theirs. I think it is wise to go into business when you are older and have had more life experiences," commented Delena. She advises others that "from the beginning, you have to have a reason to want to do something. Mine was my animals and their needs. It's great to see the benefits of good pet nutrition and be able to give back to the community. I couldn't be happier."

For more information, go to www.barkerybath.com.

STEP 2

Recognize the Opportunity
That's Right for You

CHAPTER 6

What Makes a Business Right for You?

In Step 1, What Should Baby Boomers Consider Before Starting a Business?, you looked at the big picture—of the prevalence of baby boomers starting businesses and what they should keep in mind in doing so. In Step 2, you will analyze your situation in more depth and determine what type of business fits your needs and goals.

Your One Thing

In selecting a business, you frequently hear that you need to "find your passion." It sounds great, but many people are not sure what their "passion" is. I couldn't identify mine either, initially.

It reminds me of Jack Palance in the movie *City Slickers,* as he admonished Billy Crystal to find the "One Thing" in his life that gave it meaning. When asked what the "One Thing" was, Jack Palance responded wisely that each person had to find it for himself.

As I taught others to identify their passion by looking to their past (i.e., favorite jobs, courses they loved and hobbies) and their future (their ideal life 5, 10 and 20 years down the road) the same process helped me gradually identify my own. Can you guess what? Writing! I could see signs pointing in this direction over the years—early encouragement from a college English professor (which I ignored), my love of writing new curriculum for my college courses and my enjoyment of writing entrepreneurship curriculum as a consultant. Writing was the one thing I could lose myself in and be surprised when hours rather than minutes had elapsed. I could also visualize myself in the future sitting in the sun in some warm climate with my laptop computer designing entrepreneurship curriculum or writing another book while winter raged around my midwestern home.

The business you pursue should tap into your interests and future dreams. You have probably spent way too much time working to put food on the table and send the kids to college. What captivates you? What makes you excited to get up in the morning? Now it's time to answer these questions.

Let's start the process of determining your passion by examining your dreams for the future and work backwards. I'm a big Steven Covey fan. In his book, *The Seven Habits of Highly Effective People*, I particularly like habit #2, "Begin with the End in Mind." This principle emphasizes that knowing where you want to end up provides guidance to your daily activities and enables you to accomplish your goals. To quote from Stephen Covey's Web site, (https://www.stephencovey.com/7habits/7habits-habit2.php), "If your ladder is not leaning against the right wall, every step you take gets you to the wrong place faster."

Now you will spend some time determining exactly where it is that you want to end up.

Personal Goals, Profesional Goals and Dreams

The following true story is a compelling example of the power of positive thinking and visualization in determining one's future.

At the 2000 Summer Olympics in Sydney, Australia, Maurice Greene, the track athlete, was overheard repeatedly saying to himself while preparing for a race, "I'm the fastest man in the world; I'm the fastest man in the world." Maurice Greene's father was being interviewed by a reporter nearby. Upon overhearing Maurice, he said to the reporter, "He's at it again. Maurice has been saying this since he was a little boy."

Maurice Greene obviously had the ability to dream big and visualize his success from a very young age. He was the fastest man alive that year, capturing the Olympic Gold for the 100 meter race.

What are your dreams and goals? In Action Step 6.1, you are asked to think about your future—what you would like it to be. Owning your own business is a means to achieving that end—the life you want. What does personal and professional fulfillment mean to you? What would you be doing? Enjoying? Accomplishing? What would your lifestyle be?

ACTION STEP 6.1
personal goals, professional goals and dreams

My personal and professional goals and dreams

a. Visualize what you want your personal and professional life

6.1

to be in two years. What do you see?

_____

_____

b. Visualize what you want your personal and professional life to be in five years. How old will you be?___ *(Fill in the blank.)* What do you see?

_____

_____

c. Visualize what you want your personal and professional life to be in 10 years. How old will you be? ___ *(Fill in the blank.)* What do you see?

_____

_____

d. Visualize what you want your personal and professional life to be in 20 years. How old will you be? ___ *(Fill in the blank.)* What do you see?

_____

_____

e. For the time that you will be working during the next several years, describe your ideal work setting *(i.e., What would your work environment look like? Would you be traveling? Working alone or with others? What hours would you be working?).*

_____

_____

Summary

Taking into account your responses to items a–e, summarize your personal and professional goals for the near and distant future in a couple of brief sentences.

Financial Goals

Closely aligned to your personal and professional goals are your financial goals. They likely coincide with your motivation for starting your business in the first place.

If you're struggling to pay your bills, obviously money will be more of a motivator and you will likely set your financial goals higher than if you have your financial bases covered and you are motivated by a desire to have something interesting and challenging to do. Reflect back on what you identified as your reasons for starting a business on page 43. Your definition of financial success will be significantly influenced by this motivation.

Whatever your goals, remember that money is the means to an end—the life you want—not an end in itself. With that said, however, it is important that you feel the financial rewards of having your own business are a sufficient return on your investment of dollars, time and energy. In "Financial Goals Provide Decision-Making Guidance," read how the lack of financial rewards changed one entrepreneur's mind about a particular business idea.

In Action Step 6.2, identify your financial goals as well as what assets you have available to invest in your business.

Financial Goals Provide Decision-Making Guidance. Marilyn decided to postpone her plans to start a business when she determined that the candle shop she had contemplated opening in a local strip center would not provide the income she needed to give up her job. Based on this analysis, she decided to wait until she came up with a more profitable business concept.

ACTION STEP 6.2
financial goals

Directions. Answer the following questions.

A. My financial goals

a. My *current* financial needs

I **require** the following income to support my current lifestyle. (Do *not* include what others in your household may generate.)

6.2

( ) less than $50,000 per year ( ) $ 51-$100,000 per year
( ) $101-$150,000 per year ( ) $151-$200,000 per year
( ) Over $200,000 a year

b. My *future* financial needs

I **require** the following income in the future to support my planned lifestyle and financial goals.

( ) less than $50,000 per year ( ) $ 51-$100,000 per year
( ) $101-$150,000 per year ( ) $151,000-$200,000 per year
( ) Over $200,000 a year

c. My *future* financial goals

I would **like** the following income in the future to support my planned lifestyle and financial goals.

( ) less than $50,000 per year ( ) $ 51-$100,000 per year
( ) $101-$150,000 per year ( ) $151,000-$200,000 per year
( ) Over $200,000 a year

B. My personal net worth

Answer the following questions regarding your assets and liabilities. Assets are items of value and may be liquid or fixed. Examples of liquid assets include cash *(money in checking or savings)* and near cash *(investments that can be readily converted into cash, like stocks and bonds)*. Examples of fixed assets are your home and car. Liabilities are claims against your assets, such as your home mortgage, what you owe the bank on your car.

1. My estimated liquid assets (cash/near cash) $_____
2. Other assets (estimate of real estate, cars, etc.) $_____
3. My estimated liabilities—-what I owe. $_____
4. My total net worth *$_____

   Subtract your total liabilities (3) from your total assets (1+ 2). The remainder is your net worth.

5. I am willing to invest ____ percent of my net worth in

a business. *Remember, not all of your net worth is liquid.*

6. The total amount in dollars that I am willing to invest is *$_____

6.2

Multiply your net worth, item 4, by the percentage you entered in item 5.

C. Other financial resources

In addition to what you are personally willing to invest in your business, what other funding can you obtain? Personal savings and money from family and friends are the most common sources of start-up capital. An early analysis of your personal network for potential investors / loans is helpful as you plan your business.

Source of Funding (List names)	Approximate Amount
_____	$_____
_____	$_____
_____	$_____
_____	$_____
_____	$_____
7. Total amount of money from others	$_____
8. Total amount of money from all sources	* $_____

Add together personal investment, item 6, and money from others, item 7.

SUMMARY

Taking all this information in to consideration, summarize in a couple of brief sentences your financial goals for the near and distant future.

Introduction To Featured Entrepreneur

Corporate attorney Jim Lee's examination of personal goals led him to pursue a whole new career path, providing hypnotherapy services to help people relieve or eliminate problems such as pain, stress, anxiety, insomnia and unwanted habits like smoking or overeating.

Featured Entrepreneur Jim Lee

Hypnosis for Healing
Hypnotherapy services

To some, the transition from trial lawyer to hypnotherapist may seem like a quantum leap. For Jim Lee, from Binghamton, New York, it was a small step for which he prepared for over four years by obtaining his certification in hypnotherapy and conducting sessions part time during the evenings and on weekends. When the demands on his time became too great, Jim quit his "day job," law, to devote himself full time to his business, Hypnosis for Healing.

As Jim explained, "Hypnotherapy is a safe and powerful tool to help people relieve or eliminate a variety of problems such as pain, stress, anxiety, insomnia, headaches and panic attacks or unwanted habits like smoking or overeating. Hypnotherapy is also effective in healing various physical conditions as well as promoting a sense of mental and physical well being." Jim experienced the benefits of hypnotherapy personally nine years ago when he sought relief from anxiety, which ignited his initial interest in the field.

"In law, every day was filled with confrontations with others—clients, lawyers, judges. Now every day I'm thrilled to go to the office," Jim said.

Jim went on to say, "Hypnotherapy is similar to law work as each case is different and every client is different." He reported that the questioning techniques he learned conducting pre-trial discovery and taking depositions prepared him to ask hypnotherapy clients simple questions that could not be answered with a "yes" or "no." "You ask questions to get to the root of a problem," Jim said. "Both law and hypnotherapy also involve figuring out positive suggestions to give clients and being able to think on my feet. In a session, I may have to shift at a moments notice, just like in court."

Jim currently goes to the office two to three days a week, but will expand his schedule as his client base grows. "With hypnotherapy, I rarely see someone over three sessions as most issues can be addressed in that length of time. Initially most clients were reached through my Web site. I also have developed a brochure and joined business groups to get my name out," Jim said.

Jim plans to increase business outside of his county of 200,000 by drawing from nearby cities of Syracuse (one hour away) and Rochester, New York, and Philadelphia (three hours away). "I would like to have a six-figure income in the next few years, but it is a vague goal. If I was motivated by money, I would have stayed in law," Jim stated.

As far as his plans to retire, Jim stated, "My plans are not to retire. I would never have guessed I would find something I would like so well that I would not want to retire."

For more information, go to www.hypnosisforhealing.info.

CHAPTER 7

What Do You Bring to the Table?

I'm a big believer in leading with your strengths. We all have strengths. Often we take them for granted and do not recognize their true value. In this chapter, you will identify potential businesses that capitalize on your natural abilities and the strengths you have acquired through work experiences and education or by pursuing personal interests. If you already have an idea in mind, great! This chapter gives you the opportunity to reflect on how well your business utilizes your strengths and talents.

According to Farrah Gray, a 25-year entrepreneur who made his first million dollars at age 14 and is the author of the book *Realionnaire,* successful entrepreneurship stems from defining one's area of excellence. He suggests that potential entrepreneurs answer the following questions:

- What comes easy for you and hard for others?
- What work would you do even if you were not getting paid?

- What can you give back?

I'd like to share the following story that illustrates the important of looking closely at yourself to identify where your talents lie.

Acres Of Diamonds

The story *Acres of Diamonds* has been told to hundreds of thousands over the past century, originating with Russell Herman Conwell, the founder of Temple University. I ran across the following short, simple version on the Web site of Illinois Women's Press Association (IWPA), written by Val Ensalaco:

Is the name Russell Herman Conwell familiar to you? Maybe not . . . he was born in 1843. He worked hard to earn a law degree, become a newspaper editor and later a clergyman. Dr. Conwell raised millions of dollars during his lifetime by lecturing all over the country. More than 6,000 lectures, in fact.

With the money he received, he founded Temple University with the purpose in mind of providing a place where the poor could get a quality education. At each of his lectures, he spoke of Acres of Diamonds. A true story, it goes like this:

In ancient Persia, a farmer grew wearier by the day working his land as rumors reached him of other farmers who had made millions by finding diamond mines. He sold his farm and for the rest of his life, he traveled the continent in search of diamonds. He found none. Depressed and miserable, he gave up his life by drowning himself.

Crossing a small stream, the man who bought the farmer's property spied a shiny rock lying on the bottom of the water. The prism-like reflections caught his eye. He thought the stone was a crystal and he took it to his home and placed it on the mantel. He liked looking at it.

Time passed and a visitor saw the beautiful stone and was awestruck. "Do you know what you've found?" the visitor excitedly asked. This was one of the largest diamonds ever found. The creek bottom was full of similar stones, perhaps smaller in size, but equally as brilliant.

The first farmer had owned the largest diamond field in all of Africa, but sold it for pennies on the dollar to look for diamonds in other places.

The thing about this story that so profoundly affected Dr. Conwell and, subsequently, millions of others, was the idea that each of us is, at this moment, standing in the middle of his or her own acres of diamonds. (*Reprinted with permission.*)

Each of you is standing in the middle of your own acres of "entrepreneurial" diamonds—your work experiences, skills, talents and interests. This point was reiterated in material I recently read online by Tim Barnes, entrepreneur and visiting lecturer at the Centre for Entrepreneurship at University College London. He said, "One thing that successful ideas have in common is that they are based on some form of expertise, prior knowledge or experience, or a combination of all three."

Work Experience

Work experience is the number-one source of ideas for starting a business for anyone, young or old. For the 50-plus year old, your decades of work, typically in several venues, are your acres of diamonds.

In the interviews I conducted with Featured Entrepreneurs for this book, I heard this repeated over and over again. In some cases, the business directly related to previous jobs, as was the case with Dr. James Sheehan of SchoolFinances.com. His company provides management reports and planning systems to over

150 Minnesota school districts and is the product of his years in school administration coupled with early work in computer programming. In other cases, entrepreneurs like Delena Stout of Brookside Barkery and Bath commented that almost everything she had ever done in previous jobs helped prepare her for her entrepreneurial venture.

Another reason to look to present or previous work as the inspiration for your business is that starting a new venture requires a broad range of knowledge. If you begin your entrepreneurial journey armed with technical and industry expertise, your business launch and early growth will likely go much more smoothly. As one entrepreneur put it, "Learn on someone else's checkbook." And don't underestimate the value of all those names in your address book or PDA—business contacts that may be helpful to you in identifying potential customers, employees, service providers and investors.

"Use what talents you possess: the woods would be very silent if no birds sang there except those that sang best."
Henry Van Dyke, poet

In the workplace, typically you not only learn a job, you also learn an industry. You know how your industry works and its support systems. This knowledge may very well enable you to identify business opportunities at different levels within your industry's distribution chain as well.

The Internet has dramatically altered the way some products are being distributed, flattening the distribution process and creating exciting opportunities for entrepreneurs who are now able to offer products directly to customers. Producers can reach millions by having their own Web sites or going through online vendors. The book industry is a good case in point. Many writers no longer sell through publishers but reach consumers directly through their own Web sites or through online sellers such as Amazon and Barnes & Noble.

Skills and Talents

Although many of your skills were likely acquired through work, some may be the result of self-study or trial and error. Perhaps someone mentored you along the way. Capitalizing on such expertise may be your entrepreneurial admission ticket.

Another strategy is to identify the business you want to start and work backwards, acquiring the skills and knowledge you need. You may enroll in courses or look for certain types of work opportunities. Mary Jo Troughton, featured in the following vignette "Determine Goal and Work Backwards," did both.

Determine Goal and Work Backwards. Aspiring entrepreneur Mary Jo Troughton would have been very surprised if someone had told her 10 years ago that at age 66 she would be pursuing an MBA and considering going on to a PhD.

After years as a stay-at-home mother, Mary Jo reentered the workforce at the age of 55, completing her bachelor's degree while working full time. In her work at a cancer research center, she became familiar with the grant writing process and found "the more complicated the grant, the better. In grant writing, you motivate others to provide you the information needed for the grant. You help others to see the importance of their piece to facilitate the final outcome."

To evaluate grant writing as a potential business opportunity, Mary Jo enrolled in the *FastTrac® NewVenture™* course offered by the Ewing Marion Kauffman Foundation. One piece of advice from her business coach that she particularly took to heart was to "look at the credentials of the people in the field." Noticing that most grant writers had MBAs or PhDs, Mary Jo's next step became clear: Her love of learning makes pursuing additional college coursework particularly appealing. She stated, "I receive a great amount of satisfaction from work, and plan to continue, in some capacity, indefinitely."

Hobbies and Interests

Turn something you love doing into a successful business. Now there's an entry strategy that is exciting. Many craft and hobby enthusiasts are doing just that. Thousands of discussion groups on the Internet offer support and information on how to do so.

The experience and expertise you developed during your days as a hobbyist and the contacts you made will be invaluable in your own business. A friend of mine, highlighted in "Racing Hobby Leads to Business," identified the idea for his business after years of car racing.

Technology has done a great deal to encourage the trend of turning hobbies into businesses by providing an avenue for hobbyists to sell their wares on the Internet. For as little as $10 for a domain name and a nominal fee for a Web hosting service, you can open shop, so to speak. Online craft stores and eBay® are other avenues.

Early on, you will need to realistically assess the commercial feasibility of your hobby. Will you be able to produce and sell enough to make it financially worthwhile? Are there enough potential buyers to make the business profitable?

Consider not only the hobby itself, but everything that surrounds it. For example, if you love gardening, business possibilities may include becoming a distributor of gardening supplies, teaching classes on gardening, caring for floral and plant displays in corporate office buildings or writing a gardening book.

Now you have the opportunity to revisit the three areas just discussed—work experience, skills and talents and hobbies— to see if any is a potential source of a business idea.

ACTION STEP 7.1
work experience, skills and hobbies

Follow the steps below to identify opportunities.

Step 1 Work Experiences

a. What are your current or previous work responsibilities, duties and activities?

_____

_____

b. What skills, talents, and knowledge are used to perform these work duties and responsibilities?

_____

_____

Step 2 Skills and Talents

a. What have you received positive recognition and/or awards for over your lifetime?

_____

_____

b. What would others say your skills and talents are?

_____

_____

c. On what are you considered to be an expert?

_____

_____

7.1

Step 3 Hobbies and Interests

a. What are your hobbies and interest areas?

_____

_____

b. What skills and talents do you use in your hobbies?

_____

_____

Step 4 Summary

a. Based on your answers above, what are your strengths (your diamonds)?

_____

_____

b. What potential businesses capitalize on your strengths and interests?

_____

_____

c. Of the ideas listed above, which one appeals to you the most?

_____

_____

Introduction to Featured Entrepreneur

David Polny was able to turn a hobby and passion into a classic car restoration business, 190 SL Services. He obtained expertise and assistance through the Entrepreneur Center at Sandhills Community College to help him launch his business.

Featured Entrepreneur Dave Polny

190 SL Services
Classic car restoration

Civilian life after a 20-year military career allows Dave Polny to do what others only dream of doing—restoring vintage automobiles to their original splendor. His business, 190 SL Services, specializes in full and partial restorations, servicing and repairing vintage, classic and muscle cars with a specialty in Mercedes Benz 190 SL. Located in Aberdeen, North Carolina, the business offers a full show-quality restoration that

Restored by 190 SL Services
David Preston's "Best of Show," The International 190 SL Group Concours d'Elegance
Lexington, KY - September 8, 2007

could start as high as $170,000 to $225,000, depending on the vehicle. Dave's business has attained worldwide recognition and is reached primarily through his Web site at www.190slservices.com.

"I retired from the military in December 2005," Dave stated. "I thought that if I did not get out now, I wouldn't be marketable." Dave later realized that the years he spent in Special Operations as a Green Beret helped prepare him for life as an entrepreneur. In both situations, he explained, you need to be able to think on your feet and take initiative.

Dave worked on and around cars for years prior to entering the military at 28 years old. At the young age of 13, while working at a garage on Saturdays, he learned a valuable lesson from the business's owner which he uses to this day—to rebuild rather than replace. Later, working first on Mack Trucks and then on classic cars, Dave developed his mechanical skills as well as a passion for vintage automobiles.

Connecting with the Entrepreneur Center at Sandhills Community College helped Dave develop his plans for starting a business. When the classic car restoration business for which Dave subcontracted work became available to buy, he partnered with a customer of the business to purchase it.

"There have been many lessons learned in the first few years in business," Dave stated. "There are some customers you don't want, and it's hard for new businesses to turn down work." Dave shared. He also commented that by using various planning resources, he can now complete work in 40 hours a week that initially took him 80–100 hours when he started. "The easiest thing to do is to work IN your business," he said. "It's much harder to manage your business. The work is second nature to you; management isn't."

"I make decisions differently now than I did 20 years ago," Dave reported. "Now I am as slow as a turtle in that respect. There are so many things to consider with daughters in high school and college."

When asked about retirement, Dave puts it out to 70 years of age or beyond. "I really enjoy what I am doing. I see others working longer and it keeps them alive. It keeps them going. Why quit when you are having so much fun?"

For more information, go to www.190slservices.com.

CHAPTER 8

What About Your Entrepreneurial Acumen?

Having a skill, talent or interest around which to build a business is just one part of a recipe for business success. The other is having the entrepreneurial expertise to launch, manage and grow a business. That may be the part that scares you. It is what keeps many aspiring entrepreneurs from pursuing their entrepreneurial dreams.

Entrepreneurship used to be a closed society. A person learned it around the dinner table, and if you didn't have the right people sitting at the table, you weren't sure how it worked. Luckily, colleges and even high schools today teach students entrepreneurial basics and processes; there is also much more public awareness and support for entrepreneurs as we look to them to help grow the economy.

But even with the greater general awareness of entrepreneurship, there is still some mystique surrounding it. Stories about today's entrepreneurial cult heroes only enhance the mystique. How does one compare himself to super-achievers like Bill

Gates, Steven Jobs and Michael Dell? You can't.

The list of impressive "entrepreneurial characteristics" that are included in many entrepreneurship books makes entrepreneurial success appear to require extraordinary talents and skills. Not so. Look around you. You likely know a number of successful entrepreneurs—the owner of your favorite restaurant, the health club to which you belong, or the engineering firm where you work—and they are very similar to you.

What It Takes

Let's start out by emphasizing that there is no single entrepreneurial type; and all entrepreneurs have strengths and weaknesses. So when you read the frequently cited laundry lists of entrepreneurial attributes and skills, you'll see some that you have and some you don't. Isn't that a relief?

But we need to start somewhere, and it is helpful to start out with a realistic idea of the skills, attributes and temperaments that are important to launch and grow a business. Then determine which you possess; and for those you don't, determine how much of a barrier they present and if a strategy can be developed to address the situation.

In this book, we use the word "skills" to describe abilities or proficiencies that have a strong learning component. Even though some innate aptitudes may be involved, skills typically involve coursework, training or work experience. For example, financial expertise is a skill. You may be innately good with numbers, but you still need to take financial/accounting courses or learn finances and accounting on the job to understand financial statements and be good at managing this aspect of a business.

With skills, sometimes you can get by with having a basic understanding in the area and then relying on partners, employees, contract workers or consultants to shore up your lack of in-depth expertise.

Compared to skills, attributes and temperaments—which we'll refer to as "characteristics,"—are more innate and somewhat trickier. In some cases, such as with creativity or risk taking, a partner or key management team member may bring balance to your organization. In other cases, like perseverance and determination, it's important to possess the characteristic yourself. See "Entrepreneurial Attitudes" for more information on this subject.

In the following sections, you will look at these two main categories—entrepreneurial characteristics and entrepreneurial skills. You'll determine which you possess and how to address those that are missing.

Entrepreneurial Characteristics

Entrepreneurial characteristics, or "traits" as they are frequently called, typically include a broad array of attributes and temperaments, such as creativity, self-confidence, perseverance, and so on. A common criticism of this approach is that these traits are not necessarily unique to entrepreneurs but describe many leaders and managers, as well.

For this reason, I found the 2007 study "Entrepreneurial Behavior" by Sharda Nandram and Karel Samsom particularly helpful. It overcame drawbacks of the trait approach by also looking at entrepreneurial actions. It described what successful

Entrepreneurial Attitudes. How do entrepreneurs think about themselves? The recent study, "Entrepreneurial Attitudes and Action in New Venture Development" offers some insights. The study found that positive attitudes (e.g., sense of self-efficacy, confidence and commitment) enable entrepreneurs to persist amid the uncertainty and instability of the start-up process. Another interesting finding is that there seems to be a direct association between entrepreneurial attitudes and venture performance, although this finding is not as strong. "Entrepreneurial Attitudes and Action in New Venture Development" by Rose Trevelyan, Australian School of Business, University of South Wales, as reported by the Ewing Marion Kauffman Foundation at: www.entrepreneurship.org.

entrepreneurs *do* in addition to what they *are*, and it recognized the interplay of the individual with his or her environment. *Note that Dr. Samsom, one of the authors of the study, along with his wife, Cynthia Foster, is the Featured Entrepreneur on pages 120-121.*

Nandram's and Samsom's findings indicate that to be successful, an entrepreneur must:

1. be watchful to spot the opportunities needed to start an entrepreneurial activity,
2. be persuasive in seeking cooperation or investment,
3. take time for reflection (a unique finding in terms of prior research*) in order to learn from own experiences,
4. be goal oriented in order to work efficiently,
5. be decisive,
6. be pragmatic to decrease the uncertainty and flexibility in the environment and
7. finally, have self confidence in order to face success but also failures.

Reprinted with permission.

Nandram and Samsom go on to say that needed **attributes** are (1) creativity, (2) courage, (3) trustworthiness and (4) ambition. **Temperaments** needed are (1) capacity for empathy, (2) resoluteness, (3) perseverance, (4) internal locus of control*, and (5) determination. *Internal locus of control refers to a person's perception that he or she is responsible for what happens in their lives.* Another attribute you commonly see added to this list in the literature is calculated risk taking.

In Action Step 8.1, you evaluate yourself on this criterion. I did this myself by first completing the evaluation. Then, recognizing that self-perception is not always accurate, I asked several friends and peers, as well as my husband, to assess me.

Then I summarized all responses on a blank form and averaged my scores on each item to yield a composite evaluation. This process made it easy for me to gain an overall picture of myself through respondents' eyes and allowed me to compare respondents' answers to the evaluation I completed of myself. In Action Step 8.1 you'll be asked to do the same. Now let me share with you what I learned.

Overall, my self-evaluation and those completed by others were similar, but with a few surprises. One surprise was that others ranked me much lower on "creativity" than I ranked myself. Aren't writers supposed to be creative? But then I looked at what I write—business books and instructional materials. How creative is that? It's not like I'm writing the next *Gone with the Wind*. So I guess I'll give them that. My lack of creative flair is even more apparent in the way I dress. My friends and I have a running joke about how many white blouses I own, which I have arranged in my closet according to the length of sleeve. After all, white goes with everything, right?

As an entrepreneur, you would expect that I would rate high on many of the items included, which I did. What I found helpful was identifying the items on which others rated me low. One was risk taking. Others did not perceive me as a risk taker, nor did I perceive myself as one.

As I found quite a bit of consistency among the various evaluators' responses, this gave me a clear picture of the perception others had of me. It would have been much more challenging if others' responses had been all over the board. If such were the case, I would have asked several more people to evaluate me to come up with a clearer picture of my strengths. I share this information about my assessment with the idea that doing so may demonstrate to you the benefits of completing Action Step 8.1

Once you have a clear picture of your strengths and weaknesses, what do you do with this information? It can help you determine when you need to bring others into your decision-making process or to perform certain types of work. In my case, the confirmation that I am a low risk taker helps me realize that if I err, it is usually on the side of caution. It also confirms that the type of business I own, consulting, suits me well. Knowing I don't necessarily zoom off the charts in the area of creativity encourages me to look to others to bring a creative flair to my projects as well.

Now it's time for you to complete Action Step 8.1. To obtain a more complete picture of your strengths, I suggest that you ask several friends, family members or peers to also assess you. A blank form that you can use to make copies is included on pages 254-255 of the Appendix.

8.1 ACTION STEP
entrepreneurial attributes, temperaments, behaviors
(Blank form in Appendix)

Step 1. Assess strength of each item. For each numbered item listed below, indicate the **degree** to which the attribute is possessed or exhibited by writing 1, 2, 3, 4 or 5 in the space provided.

Scale

1	2	3	4	5
absent	low	moderate	slightly high	very high

Attributes and Temperaments

___ 1. Creativity

___ 2. Courage

___ 3. Trustworthiness

___ 4 Ambition (high achievement orientation)

___ 5. Capacity for empathy

___ 6. Resoluteness

___ 7. Perseverance

___ 8. Internal locus of control (feeling you control your own destiny)

___ 9. Determination

___10. Calculated risk taker

Behaviors

___ 1. Watchful to spot the opportunities needed to start an entrepreneurial activity

___ 2. Persuasive in seeking cooperation or investment

___ 3. Takes time for reflection in order to learn from own experiences

___ 4. Goal oriented, in order to work efficiently

___ 5. Decisive

___ 6. Pragmatic, to decrease the uncertainty and flexibility in the environment

___ 7. Self-confident, in order to face success and failures

Step 2. Identify strengths. Identify those items on which you rated yourself the highest and list them here.

_____

_____

_____

8.1

8.1

Step 3. Action Step Extension. To obtain additional feedback, do the following:

A. **Obtain others' assessments.** Make copies of the blank assessment form provided on page 254-255 in the Appendix. Ask several others (family, friends, and colleagues) to assess you on the items listed and return the completed form to you.

B. **Compile results.** Copy the scores from others' assessments to a blank form. Then average the scores for each item.

C. **Identify strengths.** Identify your strengths based on how others assessed you (items with the highest averages) and list them here:

Step 4. Compare averages of assessment by others with your self-evaluation. How closely did others' perceptions of your attributes, temperaments and behaviors match your own? List any surprises here:

_____

_____

_____

_____

Step 5. Use feedback and insights. Consider how you will use the information derived through this assessment. How will insights be helpful to you in your business?

_____

_____

_____

_____

If you are interested in learning about your personal characteristics and attributes and how they compare to others in various careers, contact or visit a counseling or career center at your local college or university and inquire about assessment tools such as the Myers-Briggs Type Indicator® (MBTI) personality inventory, DISC Personality Profile or similar instruments. Some of these assessment tools are also available online.

"Many of life's failures are people who did not realize how close they were to success when they gave up."
Thomas A. Edison

Entrepreneurial Skills

In addition to the entrepreneurial attributes and characteristics identified in the previous section, there are certain skills that entrepreneurs need in order to launch and run their businesses. Many books, articles and Web sites identify these "must-have" skills, and no two lists are alike. However, there are some commonalities.

The following list of skills is based on these commonalities and my experience working with entrepreneurs. They are:
- Financial forecasting, analysis and cash flow management
- Marketing and sales—market analysis, advertising, promotion, selling and networking
- Management—planning, leadership, communications and problem solving
- Technical expertise—data processing, spreadsheet, Internet
- Operations—production, quality control and administration

Now it's time for you to evaluate which of these skills you possess, and to what degree.

8.2 ACTION STEP
entrepreneurial skills

Step 1. Rate yourself. For each numbered item listed below, indicate the **degree** to which you possess the skill by writing 1, 2, 3, 4 or 5 in the space provided.

Scale

1	2	3	4	5
absent	low	moderate	slightly high	very high

___ 1. Financial forecasting, analysis and cash flow management

___ 2. Marketing and sales—market research and analysis, advertising, promotion, selling and networking

___ 3. Management—planning, leadership, communications and problem solving

___ 4. Technical expertise—data processing, spreadsheets and Internet

___ 5. Operations—production, quality control and administration

Step 2. Identify strengths. Review how you rated yourself on the business skills above and identify which are your strengths.

_____

_____

_____

_____

Once again, you don't need to possess all these skills yourself. You will likely need to rely on the expertise of others in certain areas. Let's look at how you might strengthen or address those areas in which you rated the lowest.

STRENGTHENING WEAKNESSES

Now that you have a clearer idea of what strengths you bring to the business, you are in a position to identify what skills and abilities are still needed. Contrary to popular folklore, entrepreneurship is not a lone wolf activity; it is a team sport. Bring in other team members to perform tasks that you do not have the aptitude or experience to do well. Today, the team that supports a business may be a virtual one with members from around the country or world, e-mailing work and meeting via telephone conference calls, Webinars and virtual meetings.

In the following activity, you decide where your talents can be aptly used, what skills you need to further develop and when to look to others for missing abilities. Review Action Steps 8.1 and 8.2 in preparation for completing Action Step 8.3.

ACTION STEP 8.3
addressing gaps

1. After reviewing the strength of your attributes, behaviors and skills, which will you seek to strengthen in yourself and how will you do so?

_____

_____

_____

_____

8.3

2. Which will you seek in others?

_____

_____

_____

_____

3. How can family members and friends contribute their skills to your business?

_____

_____

_____

_____

4. What additional professional expertise (i.e., accounting, marketing, information technology, human resource management) will your business need?

_____

_____

_____

_____

> *"Often the difference between a successful man and a failure is not one's better abilities or ideas but the courage that one has to bet on his ideas, to take a calculated risk—and act."*
> Maxwell Maltz

One important and often overlooked skill for you to possess is the ability to network effectively. Let's look at this skill in more detail.

Networking—It's Who You Know

You've heard it before. It's true, and it is especially important as you start your own business. A guest speaker in one of my entrepreneurship classes, a successful entrepreneur herself, went so far as to tell students that their ability to network was one of the three skills most critical to their business success. The other two were marketing and technology.

As a Baby Boomer, the breadth and depth of your personal network sets you apart from younger entrepreneurs. Over the years, you've built a network of friends and associates to look to for ideas, information and support. It may include peers, neighbors, your banker or your doctor. It may include business colleagues, customers and suppliers. You may have met folks in volunteer situations, such as coaching your child's sports teams, or in professional or social groups—the Rotary Club or golf.

> *"Call it a clan, call it a network, call it a tribe,*
> *call it a family. Whatever you call it,*
> *whoever you are, you need one."*
> Jane Howard, *Families*

If members of your personal network are skeptical of you starting your own business, likely you will not receive the support you need to pursue this goal. If such is the case, broaden your network to include persons who are more favorably disposed to entrepreneurship, such as other entrepreneurs or business professionals who provide support to small businesses. This may involve joining an organization that has a broad and varied membership, including entrepreneurs and other business professionals, joining an entrepreneurial networking group or enrolling in an entrepreneurship course or workshop sponsored by your local college or SBA.

Building upon the network you have and honing it to include others who can contribute to your future entrepreneurial success will take attention and effort. Making the acquaintance of someone who might potentially be an important member of your entrepreneurial network is the first step. To do so, you have to get out of the house or away from your desk. Make the most of the networking opportunities you have, such as arriving early at meetings or staying afterwards to talk with people, volunteering for activities or holding an office. You also need to create new networking opportunities by joining entrepreneurial organizations and attending industry and professional meetings.

The next step in effective networking is to identify potential "networking partners," people with whom you have something in common and, potentially, can develop mutually beneficial relationships. Of course you have to get to know people, somewhat, before you can identify areas of mutual benefit. Then start building the relationship by offering to share a resource or information, or by offering to help them in some manner.

Insight or Common Sense
A successful networking relationship includes an emotional connection, reciprocity and advocacy (backing or promoting someone).

Once you start your business, networking becomes even more important, and you will also need an expanded, more formal network. This might include your accountant, attorney and banker. It may also include entrepreneurs who can mentor you and those who can help you identify and reach potential customers. Consider including such individuals on an advisory committee for your business to ensure continued contact and avail yourself of their expertise. There is much to be learned from more experienced entrepreneurs.

To learn from some of the most outstanding entrepreneurs of our time, log into Stanford University's Web site at: http://ecorner.stanford.edu

This Web site offers more than 1,200 free, high-quality podcasts and video clips of entrepreneurial thought leaders from Silicon Valley and beyond.

One final word on networking. Look closely at your personal and professional network to identify individuals with whom you can potentially partner in business. As with any business decision, the advantages and disadvantages of the partnership must be carefully considered as well as the compatibility of the partners. Common values and goals is the key to a successful partnership.

Introduction To Featured Entrepreneur

Through networking, Dr. James Sheehan identified his business partner, Ann Thomas, a former work associate, and was able to significantly grow his business, Schoolfinances.com.

Featured Entrepreneur Dr. James Sheehan

Schoolfinances.com, Inc.
Planning systems for school districts

Partners Ann Thomas and Dr. James Sheehan

A unique background as a computer programmer, teacher, principal and assistant superintendent of administrative services allowed Dr. James Sheehan to identify a need and carve out a niche for his technology-based consulting business, Schoolfinances.com, Inc. in Minnesota.

During his work career, Dr. Sheehan realized that considerable information was being collected regarding school district operations but that it was not in a format that could easily be used by school managers. He referred to such information as DRIP: Data Rich and Information Poor. This need propelled him to develop systems and reports that present data in a clear and meaningful way.

"I retired from active work in 1994," reported Dr. Sheehan. "After primarily vacationing for a few years, I began some development and sold some initial systems in 1998. I took advantage of the significant strides being made in personal computers, email and storage devices. We develop our systems in Microsoft Excel."

"I am an information monger. I had spent half my life chasing down information for superintendents or school boards—how the district compared on expenditures, salaries, and so on. I could see that a model of all of these variables would be very valuable."

The Management Reports and Planning Systems developed by Dr. Sheehan are being used in some format in over 150 of Minnesota's 340 school districts, and "many of the districts that don't use our system don't do so because they are very small," said Dr. Sheehan. He also reports that "aligning ourselves with school administrators and school boards helped." Sometimes informally referenced as the "Sheehan Model," his systems have been endorsed by the Minnesota School Boards Association (MSBA). SchoolFinances.com is also a business partner of the Minnesota Association of School Administrators (MASA). His partner, a former work associate named Ann Thomas joined the business in 2001. "She was a god-send and has allowed the business to expand with her myriad of personal skills. I have slowed down and turned more work over to Ann," Dr. Sheehan said.

"The downside of the type of business I've developed is that I can't turn it over to just anyone that walks in the door. Most of the value of the business is between our ears. I'm 71, and that's a concern. I've built a job for myself, not a business that can be readily sold," Dr. Sheehan stated.

What would Dr. Sheehan have done differently? "Had I known how interesting this would be, I probably would have quit my job earlier. But people want to see someone a little older and with more experience consulting. Some people are reluctant to secure consulting services from young people."

Dr. Sheehan recommends that individuals looking to start their own businesses do something about which they are passionate, as "you frequently end up working 14–16 hours a day, at least initially." He estimates that he spent over 3,000 hours developing the Minnesota school district Financial Planning Model. He also says, "Do something in the area you have spent your life getting some experience."

For more information, go towww.schoolfinances.com.

CHAPTER 9

What the Marketplace Tells You

In the previous chapters, you mainly looked inward, at your skills, work experiences and interests. You also determined what entrepreneurial skills and characteristics you possessed and what actions to take to shore up those that needed strengthening.

In the following chapters you will look outward, at the marketplace, either for business ideas or for market confirmation that the idea you have is a good one.

Remember the story, "Acres of Diamonds," in Chapter 7? It was about a poor farmer in ancient Persia who sold his farm and spent the rest of his life traveling the continent looking for diamonds. Unknowingly, he had sold the largest diamond field in all of Persia and spent the rest of his life looking for diamonds elsewhere.

Had the farmer taken the time to learn what rough diamonds looked like and carefully explored his own property, he would have been wealthy beyond his wildest dreams. Similarly, you will want to know when a business idea is a winning one, an entrepreneurial diamond.

A Winning Business Idea

A winning business idea satisfies a market need, plain and simple. In other words, the marketplace determines whether or not a business idea is a winner. You have only to look around you to see how the marketplace affects a business's success. For example, an Italian restaurant may thrive in one area of the city but fail dismally in another. Construction in one area of the country may be booming and be at a dead standstill in another.

If you don't yet have an idea for your business, you can start with the marketplace and identify what is needed. If you already have an idea, this is a good time to analyze the marketplace for confirmation that your business idea fills a need. In either instance, it is about the marketplace.

Identify a Marketplace Need

Since marketplace needs are the diamonds you are seeking, how can you improve your odds of spotting them? The best way is to adopt an entrepreneurial mindset. Entrepreneurs look to solve a problem, fill a niche or remedy a performance gap in the marketplace.

- **Solve a problem.** Entrepreneurs see problems as opportunities. Delena Stout, of Brookside Barkery and Bath (page 69), came up with her idea as a result of the problem she experienced trying to find a place to wash her large dogs. Addressing this problem and capitalizing on consumers' interest in healthy, natural and holistic pet foods, Delena launched Brookside Barkery and Bath, which has since grown to three locations.
- **Fill a market niche.** Large businesses typically focus on mass markets. This provides a great opportunity for small business to focus on niche markets. Dave Polny's business,

Solve a Problem

Upon moving to the United State, Penelope experienced difficulty obtaining food items from her native country and found others did as well. She started a small retail shop to import and sell these items to others in her community, who, like her, longed for the "taste of home."

190 SL Services (page 91), identified a need that was not being addressed by mainstream providers. He specializes in full and partial restorations and servicing vintage and classic cars with a specialty of Mercedes Benz 190 SLs. Customers come from around the country.

Read "Something for Everyone" for another example of a business fulfilling a niche market.

- **Fill a performance gap.** Small businesses are nimble and quick. Working close to the customer, they are often the first to spot opportunities where customers are being poorly served. Dr. James Sheehan found that school district administrators were Data Rich and Information Poor—DRIP as he referred to it. Considerable information was collected regarding school district operations, but it was not in a format that could be easily used by school managers. This gap propelled Dr. Sheehan to start his business, Schoolfinances.com (page 108), providing systems and reports that present data in a clear and meaningful way to school districts.

- **Fulfill a customer want.** Small businesses' close proximity to the customer gives them a competitive advantage by affording them the opportunity to provide excellent customer service and/or unique or customized products. Featured Entrepreneur Bill VendeBerghe and his wife Vicki (page 23) adopted a business strategy for Fox Hill Farm Leather that was different than that of their larger wholesale competitors—not requiring a minimum purchase. This enabled them to service small accounts that were not served by larger suppliers. Their one-stop shopping site for small retailers has worked well, and their wholesale business makes up 85 percent of their sales.

Something for Everyone. On the extreme end of the niche world of dating sites is MulletPassions.com. Businesses competing with companies such as Match.com or eHarmony are seeing more success targeting those with specific interests; hence sites like Golfmates.com and SingleParent.com. "A Dating Site for Everyone" by Ellen McCarty, The Washington Post

Velcro Invention—A Walk in the Park. George Mesral, the inventor of Velcro, demonstrated an entrepreneurial mindset as he walked through the woods and noticed how cockleburs caught in his clothes and in his dog's fur. An engineer by trade, he decided to examine why they stuck so tightly. His observation and investigation led to the development of Velcro.* How many others had the same experience but failed to see the possibilities in what they observed?
*The History of VELCRO® and Velcro Products. http://www.troyerproducts.com/velcrohistory.asp

Insight or Common Sense

A simple technique like noting products available elsewhere but not at home is a way of turning your travels into entrepreneurial adventures.

Now let's look at some techniques to help you spot marketplace problems, niches, and gaps elsewhere. To do so, you need to raise your antennae to pick up marketplace signals. The following activities will help you.

• **Listen** to people around you—friends, family, colleagues, customers. What are they saying? Complaining about? What problems are they experiencing?

• **Read** magazines, newspapers and books and scan the Internet. What trends are they identifying? What topics are they addressing?

• **Observe** the world around you. Read in "Velcro Invention—A Walk in the Park" how engineer George Mesral's observation skills led to the creation of Velcro. Howard Schultz, the founder of Starbucks, is another example of how important observation skills are to entrepreneurial success. On a visit to Milan, Italy, Schultz noted the coffee culture in the local coffee shops and later sought to recreate this "socializing" experience for patrons of Starbucks.

• **Research** trends and changes in government regulations and technology innovations. Identifying trends early gives entrepreneurs the opportunity to offer their products and services before the competition is strong. Change creates disruption, and disruption creates gaps and unmet needs that entrepreneurs can address.

Browse the Web to identify trends related to your particular area of interest or industry. For example, if you have an interest in technology, you may want to visit Xconomy.com for technology news and trends. On this Web site, you can view the list of businesses being funded by venture capitalists. Type "venture capital funding" in the Search box. Looking at these businesses being funded can help you anticipate which areas are growing. Similar Web sites exist in other industries.

> *"I'm a great believer in luck, and I find the harder I work, the more I have of it."*
> Thomas Jefferson

In Action Step 9.1, you identify potential business ideas by carefully observing the marketplace. In Action Step 9.2, you narrow your focus to the industry in which you are interested to spot opportunities that may exist there.

9.1
ACTION STEP
marketplace analysis

Keep a log of possible ideas by tuning in to your environment. Look closely at the marketplace. What problems have you experienced? What frustrations have you observed others experiencing or have you heard others talk about? What opportunities are identified in magazines or newspapers?

Idea	Source of Idea	How Idea Was Identified
Brief description of idea	Need? Want? Problem? Frustration?	Personal observation? Talking with others? Magazine or News-paper Article? (Date)
example: In-Home care for aging	*example*: Personal Need	*example*: Talking with others, personal

Yours:

	Idea	Source of Idea	How Idea was Identified
1.	_____	_____	_____
	_____	_____	_____
2.	_____	_____	_____
	_____	_____	_____
3.	_____	_____	_____
	_____	_____	_____

9.2 ACTION STEP
industry analysis

As a framework for answering the following questions, use the industry in which you currently work or in which you have spent most of your work career.

1. Are there products or services that are needed or wanted and are currently unavailable? If so, what?

_____

_____

2. Is there a lack of high quality options for certain products or services? If so, what?

_____

_____

3. Can you improve upon a product or service that is currently being offered? If so, how?

9.2

_____

_____

4. Is there a market niche with needs that are being overlooked? If so, what niche?

_____

_____

5. Is there a need for more providers of a certain type of product or service? If so, what?

_____

_____

Now you have identified some problems, gaps, or niche markets. This is your chance to put all those years of life and work experience to good use in developing a product or service to fulfill the needs and gaps you have observed, not just in the same ho-hum way others do it, but by using your own creative flair. After all, you are unique and bring a combination of work and life experiences to the table that no one else in the universe has. Here's your chance to shine.

A Dash of Creativity

Everyone is creative in some way. When people say they aren't, they are usually thinking of creativity in an artistic sense—visual and performing arts, writing. It's more likely that you exhibit your creativity in the way you live your everyday life, solving problems in new and different ways.

I recall an entrepreneur in one of my workshops saying he was about as creative as a "rock." He then went on to talk about his ability to walk into an older home and envision how removing walls and adding windows would update and open the space to appeal to the contemporary home buyer.

With thousands of new products failing each year, use your creativity to be an innovator rather than an inventor. Consider changing and improving something already in the marketplace rather than introducing something new. Innovation increases the value proposition for the consumer—what they get in exchange for what they pay.

"First comes thought; then organization of that thought into ideas and plans, then transformation of those plans into reality. The beginning, as you will observe, is your imagination."
Napoleon Hill

And you don't necessarily have to come up with something new for your business to succeed. In *The Origin and Evolution of New Business*, Amar Bhidē notes that most entrepreneurs start businesses by copying or slightly modifying someone else's idea.

It is the simple, even mundane ideas that typically represent the greatest chance of success. Adding a dash of creativity to a tried-and-true concept may give you the marketplace edge you need.

Innovation in Services. A large percentage of business today involves services, estimated to account for 70 percent of the U. S. Gross Domestic Product. A recent report in Great Britain describes three big changes affecting service industries:

1. The convergence of manufacturing and service innovation where many firms add a "service wrapper" (e.g. post-sales maintenance and support) to the sale of a manufactured product;
2. The growing role of users and consumers in the innovation process; and,
3. Growing concerns about sustainability and the environment.

Source: Department of Business Enterprise and Regulatory Reform, United Kingdom. For the complete report, Supporting Innovation in Services, go to: www.berr.gov.uk/files/file47440.pdf.

Regarding innovation, Peter Drucker suggests in *Managing for Results* that entrepreneurs

- Keep it simple, keep it focused.
- Start small – try to do one specific thing.

In addition to product/service innovation, you can distinguish your business by being creative in your marketing, packaging or distribution methods. One technique for getting out of your box, so to speak, is to combine things that do not normally go together. Try this technique yourself. Look at how products or services are marketed, packaged or distributed in other industries and apply those techniques to your products or services.

I recently read about a jewelry company that has been very successful doing just this. Silpada Designs, which has grown to over a thousand sales representatives in the last 10 years, sells sterling silver jewelry through home parties, a sales technique more commonly associated with Tupperware and Pampered Chef kitchen products. Read "Innovation in Services" for information about new directions in services.

Now try your hand at applying a dash of creativity to your product or service in *Pause & Reflect*.

For an extensive listing of resources on innovation and creativity, including numerous short videos by leading authorities in the field, go to www.edcorner.stanford.edu. Under "Topics," click on "Creativity and Innovation."

Introduction To Featured Entrepreneur

Venice Beach Eco Cottages aren't your run-of-the-mill tourist cottages. Read how entrepreneur Cynthia Foster and husband, Karel Samsom, used their unique talents to create "green" eco-friendly cottages as a beloved art project.

Pause & Reflect
What changes can you make to your product or service to set it apart from others in the marketplace?

_____

_____

_____

_____

_____

_____

_____

_____

How can you creatively market, package or distribute your product or service?

_____

_____

_____

_____

_____

_____

_____

Featured Entrepreneur Cynthia Foster

Venice Beach Eco Cottages
Eco-friendly cottages in Venice Beach

Cynthia Foster in cottage

Cynthia Foster, along with husband Dr. Karel Samsom, a professor of environmental entrepreneurship at Nyenrode Business Universiteit in the Netherlands, co-owns Venice Beach Eco Cottages, in Venice Beach, California. When Cynthia met Karel seven years ago, she had no idea how much her life would change. It was also the day she contracted Lyme disease.

Cynthia describes her life up until that point as "linear." She had owned a business management practice in the film and music business in Los Angeles for 16 years with high-profile directors and producers as clients. Her work life was extremely high pressure. Every hour of the day was tightly scheduled, and the work itself was all left brain.

Health issues resulting from Cynthia's Lyme disease initially did not allow her to work, resulting in the loss of her business and home. In hind-sight, Cynthia refers to this as a freeing experience that allowed her to explore other ways of working and creating from both sides of her brain – the linear left and the spirally right. For the last seven years, Cynthia has been immersed in creative pursuits, working as an actor in film, theater and television, and renovating properties on the side with husband, Karel.

Selling an investment property in Vermont initially caused Karel and Cynthia to search for properties in California that they could renovate, offering guests the type of urban retreat they sought in the individual homes they preferred in their frequent travels. After months of searching, they found the ideal properties: three 1922 bungalows that came on the market, next door to the cottage they were renting in Venice Beach.

All went well until a few days before their scheduled closing on the properties, when their construction loan fell through as a result of the credit meltdown. After a careful analysis of their options, Cynthia and Karel decided to self finance the cottages' renovations by accessing a portion of Karel's 401K. As it happened, the timing worked well: It occurred just prior to the stock market plummet during the summer and fall of 2008.

This husband-wife team blended their respective backgrounds as an environmental economist and an actor/artist to create the cottages as a beloved art project, carefully preserving the old-Venice architecture of the area. Cynthia was also inspired by her childhood summer vacations at a small Wisconsin lake resort of one- and two-bedroom cabins owned by her grandmother.

In addition to their beauty and comfort, the Venice Beach cottages are healthy for guests and the planet. All building materials are sustainable and non-toxic, all paints and finishes have no/low VOCs, linens and mattresses are organic, and cleaning supplies are all natural and fragrance free. In addition, the cottages are solar-powered with great electronics and only four blocks from the beach.

The only marketing to date has been an initial investment in public relations to launch the business. That and the eco-friendly nature of the cottages resulted in extensive publicity—The New York Times, Los

Cynthia and Karel

Angeles Magazine, Hospitality Design—The Green Issue, Elle, Travel Agent Magazine, The Sundance Channel's "Big Ideas for a Small Planet" TV Show, TreeHugger.com., etc. Visits also offer guests a chance to "do good" while feeling good, as three percent of the revenue from each visit goes to charity.

For more information, go to: www.venicebeachecocottages.com.

Step 1 What Should Baby Boomers Consider Before Starting a Business?

Step 2 Recognize the Opportunity That's Right for You and the Marketplace

Step 3 Refine Your Idea and Do Your Research

Step 4 Determine Business Viability and Get Started

CHAPTER 10

Timing Is Everything

You've heard this cliché before. But when it comes to business, it's definitely true. Your timing in entering the market is critical to the success of your business.

Trends—Catch The Wave

Do you know the difference between a trend and a fad? A *trend* refers to a general direction or tendency over a period of some duration, which provides a fairly substantial window of opportunity for entrepreneurs, which is the time you have to act on an opportunity or it will be missed. *Fads*, on the other hand, are of shorter duration and provide a shorter timeframe for acting. Synonyms of "fad" are "craze" and "whim."

The short-term nature of businesses based on fads or one-time events may be viewed as an advantage by some entrepreneurs. It may provide short-term profits without a long-term commitment to running a business. For example, many businesses have sprung up around Olympic Games, significant anniversaries of cities or states, holidays or the success of local

Fads Can Be Risky. In Andrew's specialty store, his best-selling product line was a popular, collectible, children's stuffed toy. When customers' interests waned, sales significantly declined resulting in considerable financial hardship because of his dependence on this one product group.

sports teams. Vendors literally pop up on every street corner. Around here, the nearby university's basketball team generates a tremendous amount of excitement and loyalty, especially during March Madness, the NCAA men's basketball tournament. University memorabilia is at a premium during that time.

Awareness of the short-term nature of these opportunities is the key. Read about one entrepreneur's challenges as a result of depending too heavily on fad merchandise in his store in "Fads Can Be Risky."

Most businesses, however, capitalize on trends, which provide a more solid foundation for growth. This is the philosophy of catching the wave early and riding it until it crests. But to do so, you need to see it coming.

If you don't have a business idea, spotting major trends and their related marketplace needs can be a way to identify an idea for a potential business. If you already have a business in mind, identifying relevant trends may help you fine-tune your business concept to take advantage of them.

A few years ago, a friend of mine spent months researching the demand for self-storage units prior to building a climate- and non-climate-controlled storage center. In his research, he uncovered supportive trend data related to the mobility of the U.S. population and the increasing number of possessions people accumulated and didn't always have room for, which convinced him that there was a strong need for this type of business.

Some entrepreneurs reverse the process and first identify major trends and then look for related business opportunities. For instance, had my friend first identified the increased mobility of the U.S. population, he might have then identified the need for self-storage units.

In her book *Clicking, 17 Trends That Drive Your Business—*

And Your Life, Faith Popcorn emphasizes the need for a business to be "on trend" in multiple areas. Sometimes even minor adaptations to be "on trend" can reap significant results. For example, several national restaurant chains have added healthy, low-calorie menu items to address the growing awareness of our society's obesity problem. Others have added menu "value" items for the cost-conscious consumer.

Finding Information on Trends

Information on trends abounds in newspapers, magazines, radio, TV, Web sites, trade shows, the list goes on and on. *Entrepreneur* and *Business Start-Up* magazines, among others, identify trends in entrepreneurship. Among "2009 Trends to Watch" at *Entrepreneur Magazine's* Web site (http://www.entrepreneur. com/hottrends) are going green (organics, clean energy), health and fitness, and products and services that appeal to Boomer lifestyles and stages—Boomers are downsizing and 1/3 are single head of household.

> *"Prediction is difficult, especially about the future."*
> Yogi Berra

At the time of this writing, a search for books using the keyword "trends" on Amazon.com resulted in a listing of over 475,000 books! A search for "demographic trends" yielded more than 15,000 titles. A visit to your local library will leave you buried in resources. Industry associations and their trade shows and conventions are also an excellent source of information on latest industry specific trends. Visiting the Web site www.trendwatching.com is a way to keep abreast of consumer trends.

Be a trend spotter in your daily life by observing what's going on in your community and others. Your travels throughout the United States and internationally may alert you to trends that are likely to impact your local area down the road. For example, New York and Los Angeles are known for their fashion forwardness, the West Coast for technology.

> *"Don't skate to the puck; skate to where*
> *the puck is going to be."*
> Wayne Gretzsky, hockey player

With so much information available on trends, identifying trend categories can be helpful. Major categories examined in this chapter include technology, demographic, economic and social. To find out more, google "demographic trends," "social trends," "economic trends," or "technology trends" in quotation marks. You will be provided a long list of resources. Now, we'll explore each major trend area in more depth.

Demographic Trends

Demographics drive the demand for most consumer products and services, which, in turn, drive the demand for most business products. Therefore, the more you know about the demographics of the marketplace in general and your target market in particular, the better. For consumer markets, demographic variables include factors such as age, gender, income, education and ethnicity. See the following table for more specifics about age demographics in the United States.

Identifying the demographic age group of your targeted customers is an easy way to find out about their general buying habits, lifestyles, mindsets and needs. Using your favorite search engine, enter the term from column one that best describes your

Generations* Based on 2005 U.S. Census	Birth years* Note: Some overlap exits between groups	Approximate Population Size
World War II	1931	20 million
Swing Generation	1932-1944	28 million
Baby Boomers	1945-1953 Leading edge Boomers 1954-early '60s Younger Boomers	75 million
Generation X (Gen X)	1964 through late '70s	50 million
Generation Y (Millennials, Echo-Boomers)	1980s through mid '90s	73 million

target market (i.e., Gen X, Baby Boomers). You'll be directed to a wealth of information.

Shifting age demographics and consumer needs influenced by age can be predicted decades in advance. The massive Boomer generation had a significant impact on the need for public schools in the '50s, the housing market in the '70s and '80s and consumer spending and savings in the last several decades.

Many successful businesses resulted from entrepreneurs anticipating the needs and wants of this massive group of buyers. As Boomers age, the impact will be felt in the areas of changing housing needs, health care and elder services, to name a few. *Hint. Hint. Are there potential businesses here?*

Now it's time for you to try your hand at identifying significant demographic trends in Action Step 10.1.

10.1 ACTION STEP
demographic trends

Using your favorite Internet search engine, type in "demographic trends" and browse the listing of resources, or scan magazines and newspapers. Visit the library for additional resources. After identifying trends you find of particular interest, brainstorm potential business ideas related to them.

Demographic Trend	Source of Information	Opportunities
Examples: The number of Hispanics in the population profile of the U.S. has more than doubled since 1980	U.S. Census Bureau, 2008	Hispanic-oriented magazines, newspapers, grocery stores, restaurants, translation services for employers
Increased number of people living into their late 80s and 90s	Observation, U.S. Census Bureau	Elder services, senior friendly homes, aging-in-place products

Yours:

1. _____ _____ _____

   _____ _____ _____

2. _____ _____ _____

   _____ _____ _____

3. _____ _____ _____

   _____ _____ _____

Technology Trends

Several decades ago, renowned economist Joseph Shumpeter coined the term "creative destruction," to describe how the same innovation that creates opportunity for one business sometimes destroys another. This is especially true with technology.

For example, the Internet has changed the way businesses advertise and sell their products and how consumers purchase them. It has also created many opportunities for small businesses to have a large presence in the virtual world. Read about today's technology trends in "Hottest Technology Trends."

Can you spot any opportunities resulting from recent technology advances? In Action Step 10.2 you'll be asked to identify those you noted.

> *"If you are not early, you are late."*
> John R. Ortego

Hottest Technology Trends. eWeek.com included these trends on its list of those to watch:

- Cloud computing (a way to access enterprise class technology with minimal upfront costs),
- Notebook/Netbook adoptions (which outpaced desktop sales), and
- Social networking (LinkedIn, FaceBook, Twitter).

Read more at: www.eweek.com/c/a/Midmarket/Five-Tech-Trends-to-Watch-in-2009/

Economic Trends

In the last several years, we have been through some exciting economic times. For example, the Dow Jones Industrial Average fell over 700 points on September 28, 2008, and rose over 900 points on October 13, 2008. I have a feeling the excitement isn't over yet. We also saw a housing market bust, the fall of several major financial institutions and an overhaul of our credit markets, which had a significant impact on both consumers and businesses as financial institutions tightened their lending programs. Even as the economy recovers, it's challenging to keep up with all the news.

It's important to stay abreast of news that most directly affects your potential business. For industry-specific information, trade associations can be a very helpful. If you are not aware of an association related to your type of business, google "trade associations" "xxx," substituting your type of business for the "xxx."

Social Trends

As Baby Boomers, we've seen a lot of social changes in our life time. These changes spawned many new products and services in the marketplace. For example, when more women began working outside the home in the '60s and the subsequent four decades, support services emerged, including day care, housecleaning, and growth of fast-food restaurants. Today, the trend of women working outside of the home has stalled or maybe reversed, which will have an impact in the marketplace in the future.

A more recent trend, that of more people now living alone (young people marrying later, divorces, people living longer) has produced an array of marketplace responses such as small-portion food packaging, maintenance provided communities and doggie day-care services.

Now it's your turn. List trends you have identified in Action Step 10.2 and explore related business opportunities.

10.2 ACTION STEP
technical, economic and social trends

After scanning the Internet and various printed sources for trends in general or in your particular area of interest, identify significant trends and brainstorm business ideas related to them.

Trend	Source of Information	Opportunities
Example: Social Trend—Gen X and Y having larger families than Baby Boomers	wbsonline.com	Day care and nanny services, child taxi services, tutoring, child products

10.2

Yours:

1._____   _____   _____

_____   _____   _____

2._____   _____   _____

_____   _____   _____

3._____   _____   _____

_____   _____   _____

Tweaking Business to be On Trend

If you have a business already in mind, how can you adapt it to be more in tune with one or more of the trends you identified?

Product/Service Life Cycle

Just like us, products go through a life cycle. Understanding this can be very helpful to entrepreneurs as they consider whether or not it is a good time to enter a market. The stage at which products are in their life cycle has a significant impact on a business's chances of success.

Life cycles vary tremendously in length. Short life cycle products include fashion, some toys (especially ones based on the latest movie releases) and many technology-based products. By comparison, furniture, jewelry and food products have a much longer life cycle.

The stages in a product's life cycle (PLC) include introduction, growth, maturity and decline. Identifying your product's stage helps you anticipate opportunities and challenges.

- **Introduction Stage.** When new products are first introduced into the marketplace, they typically require extensive amounts of capital for educating the market and promotion. At this stage, you are pioneering the way, and pioneering takes time and money—two things that Baby Boomers are frugal about. Because of these high expenses, it is difficult for a business to be profitable at this stage.

- **Growth Stage**. At this stage, customers are knowledgeable about the product and are ready to buy. The marketplace increasingly demands more, and room exists for additional providers. "Green" environmental products for the home and in clothing are current examples. This stage, with its high demand and profit margins, generally provides the greatest opportunities for new businesses. You can "catch the wave," so to speak. The earlier you catch it, the longer the ride.
One important consideration at this stage and the next, maturity, is whether or not you will be able to set your business apart from others in the market.

- **Maturity Stage**. Here demand remains relatively stable or decreases. More and more providers are meeting the needs of customers, which often results in aggressive competition and price cutting. The fast food industry is a good example. Because of many large and well established competitors, small businesses will likely need to specialize in a particular area or focus on smaller niche markets. Personal customer service, an advantage that small businesses can have over their larger counterparts, is another key to attracting and keeping customers at this stage.

- **Decline Stage.** This stage is characterized by decreasing product demand and producers leaving the marketplace. Greeting cards and stationery stores are current examples. In the decline stage, many providers are exiting, not entering, the market. At this stage, you should seriously question entering the market at all. Why would you want to swim upstream? Why not look for a business that you can catch the wave **before** it crests? In some situations, however, research may reveal that there is still growth potential in a specific trade area, running counter to the declining demand in a regional or national market.

Today product life cycles are becoming increasingly shorter as change is occurring at an ever increasing rate of speed. In other words, your window of opportunity is getting shorter, which results in a need to adapt and change frequently or quickly. Knowing where your product is in its life cycle enables you to make the most of the opportunity presented and anticipate when change is needed.

In Action Step 10.3, you consider where your business's main product or service is in its life cycle.

ACTION STEP 10.3
product/service life cycle

Answer the questions below.

a. Based on your knowledge or research of the product/service you will be offering, where is it in its life cycle in the trade area

10.3

in which you plan to operate: Introduction? Growth? Maturity? Decline?

_____

_____

_____

b. What evidence do you have that your main product or service is at this stage?

_____

_____

_____

c. What challenges do you anticipate at this stage in your product's/service's life cycle?

_____

_____

_____

Step 2 Conclusion: Recognize The Opportunity

Now it's time to take stock. You've worked through Step 2, Recognize the Opportunity. You have a good sense of what an entrepreneurial diamond looks like, and you have examined your skills and abilities as well as the marketplace for possible diamonds. You may have come up with a number of business ideas or gained clarity on the appropriateness of the one with which you started. In Action Step 10.4, you'll describe your idea.

Briefly describe the business idea about which you are most excited and that you feel presents the greatest opportunity.

_____

_____

_____

_____

_____

_____

_____

_____

Now you are ready to fine-tune this idea and start your research to evaluate it for feasibility, which you will do in Step 3.

Introduction To Featured Entrepreneur

Terrie Boguski was able to "catch the wave," the trend toward environmental conservation. This resulted in work waiting for her when she started her environmental consulting business. Read about Terrie's entrepreneurial journey in the following.

Featured Entrepreneur Terrie Boguski

Harmony Environment LLC
Environmental consulting

Terrie Boguski,
Harmony Environment LLC

When her employer of 10 years announced that employees should start looking for jobs, Terrie Boguski found herself in a quandary. With a degree in chemical engineering and a master's in environmental engineering, Terri had been fortunate to be able to do most of her work out of her home during the 10-year time period she had worked for her employer. "I didn't want to upset my way of life and work in an office. Finding employment would necessitate a significant change in my lifestyle," she stated. The prospects of having to find a job and go to an office every day were deciding factors in Terrie's decision to start her own business

At 50 years old, with her three children raised for the most part and her husband in a secure job, Terrie decided that she could weather the risks of self-employment, a luxury she had not had in her younger years. From work experience in the field and a comment by a former employer, an environmental consultant, the idea for her business took root. "He told me to come to him first if I decided to start my own business, and I did," Terrie commented.

Terrie started Harmony Environmental LLC in October 2007 on a part-time basis, continuing to work for her employer as she gained experience and confidence in her entrepreneurial venture's ability to sustain itself. Harmony conducts life cycle assessments and green house gas emissions inventories (carbon footprints) for clients. "The time is right for this type of work—work was waiting for me when I started," Terrie said. "Now I have more work than I can handle." The low start-up costs also contributed to making this type of business attractive.

"I thought of having my own business off and on over the years, but I was busy with family—three children. Self employment is working well for me," states Terrie. "I plan to stay the same for a few more years. If I want to take on more work, I will subcontract. Taking on employees means taking on responsibilities for others' livelihoods, and I am not ready for that."

In looking toward the future, Terrie commented, "I think having your own small business as you approach retirement enables you to weather the ups and downs better than if you work for someone else, especially if it is the type of business where you can adjust the workload to fit your need for personal time."

You can reach Terrie at: tboguski@harmonyenviro.com.

STEP 3

Refine Your Idea and Do Your Research

CHAPTER 11

From Fuzzy to Finite

By now, the business idea that has been hovering in your mind for months, or maybe years, has started to come clearly into focus. Or perhaps you were fairly clear about it from the start, and your work thus far has confirmed that it is what you want to do. Your business is exciting to think about and may be the key to your future.

But slow down. Let's ask a few basic questions about your proposed business:

- What will you sell?
- Who will buy from you?
- How will you market your products and services?

It's OK to be a little fuzzy right now. But if you are **totally** in the dark about the answers to these questions, take a moment and reflect on whether or not you have the knowledge and expertise to pull this off, or the commitment to obtain it.

What benefits are
your intended cus-
tomers seeking?

——————————

——————————

——————————

——————————

——————————

——————————

——————————

——————————

What product/service
features would pro-
vide these benefits?

——————————

——————————

——————————

——————————

——————————

——————————

——————————

——————————

What Will You Sell?

Answering this question appears easy. You, like a lot of entrepreneurs, have likely focused on conceptualizing your product
or service. And you, like a lot of entrepreneurs, have probably
thought long and hard about what features you will offer in your
products or services.

The problem is, however, that customers don't buy features;
they buy benefits. They buy from you because your products/
services provide the benefits they are seeking. It's easy for entrepreneurs to become enthralled with all the features they can
include and to assume that the customer will value the features
as much as they do. Wrong!

Take me, for example. I have a cell phone with a keyboard
for text messaging, which I don't do; the ability to play music,
which I don't use; and a camera, which has only been used when
I accidentally hit a button and took a picture of the floor. I have
yet to personally see the value of any of these features.

Then why did I buy the phone? Almost by accident, the
sales clerk commented that I would be able to access e-mails
while traveling. Bingo! That was a benefit I valued. He made
the sale.

Benefits are the product's advantages to the buyer. They
are where you start in designing your product/service. Identify
what benefits your potential customers are seeking and then
work backwards to include features that provide them. In *Pause
& Reflect*, you will do so for the main product or service you
intend to sell.

Seriously question the wisdom of providing features that
have little benefit to most of your customers. Just because you
are captivated with features doesn't mean that your customer

will be, and they certainly won't want to pay more for features of little or no value to them personally.

"Go with the simple."
Albert Einstein

Now is a good time to take a step back, look at the marketplace, see what benefits and features customers want, and, if necessary, modify your product to include those benefits and features BEFORE launching your business.

What Winners Can Tell You

Winners in the marketplace, in general, and in your field, in particular, can tell you what customers value, what sells and what doesn't—what benefits customers are seeking and what features provide them.

Look for successful businesses you can emulate. Using our economic superstars as an example, consider companies such as Microsoft, Coca-Cola, Starbucks, and Walmart, to name a few. What makes these businesses successful? If you thought of things like a quality product, excellent customer service, convenient locations, effective marketing and a fair value exchange for your dollar, you are right on track. We'll call these Critical Success Factors (CSFs).

CSFs vary by type of business. For example, speed in product preparation may be a CSF for a local coffee shop but not for the upscale restaurant where patrons expect a leisurely dining experience. Location may be a CSF for a print shop but isn't as important for an accountant. Recently, I heard Herb Kelleher, co-founder of Southwest Airlines, interviewed on television. He commented that Southwest Airlines' success is due to the business model which they introduced in the airline industry

Insight or Common Sense
Additional features typically add costs, and higher costs result in higher prices to customers. Make sure the cost of any feature is outweighed by its benefit to the customer.

Pause & Reflect
What are the Critical
Success Factors for
your type of busi-
ness?

_____

_____

_____

_____

_____

_____

_____

_____

decades ago—low prices, better service and an atmosphere of fun. Kelleher also commented that despite being an open book about their success, no other airline had duplicated it. My question to you is, "Why not?"

Successful companies have figured out what their CSFs are Now is your opportunity to do the same in the Pause & Reflect activity which follows.

To explore the concept of Critical Success Factors further, focus on successful competitors in your field and learn from them. Don't fall into the trap of discounting the abilities of your competitors. Remember, companies that have been in business for a while are meeting customers' needs at some level, or they would not be in business. Analyze your competitors, emulating their strengths and remedying their weaknesses to put your business on the fast track to success.

Action Step 11.1 poses important questions to consider in analyzing competitors. Complete this activity for each of your key competitors. A blank form is included in the Appendix on page 254 for you to copy in order to do so.

11.1 ACTION STEP
learning from key competitors
(Blank form in Appendix)

Check your local Yellow Pages, search the Internet, or talk to people to identify successful businesses offering products/services similar to yours. Then find out as much as you can about these businesses. If they are retail establishments in your area, visit them. If not, gather information through literature and the Internet or by talking to customers and vendors. Then answer the following questions for each:

11.1

a. Name and location of business

_____

_____

b. Description of product(s) or service(s)

_____

_____

c. What are their best sellers?

_____

_____

d. What is the business doing right?

_____

_____

e. How can aspects of the business be improved?
   (There is always room for improvement.)

_____

_____

Repeat this activity for all key competitors.

Who Will Buy From You— Target Markets

"Target markets" is a term with which you'll become very familiar. It alludes to market segmentation—the concept that a mass
market can be divided into segments with identifying charac-

teristics. For example, the homeowner market can be broken down into very distinct target markets with very different needs: first-time home buyers, families with children, empty nesters, senior citizens and so on.

By very specifically identifying your target market, you can ensure that your product/service meets their needs. You can also be more effective in promoting your products or services to potential customers as you can more clearly determine how to reach them.

Most successful small businesses target specific markets, as opposed to mass marketing, which is often used by large businesses. It's one way small businesses can successfully compete against their much larger counterparts.

Anytime an entrepreneur tells me that **"everyone"** is his or her intended market, I cringe. I interpret the entrepreneur's comment to say, "I don't really know who will purchase my product/service." What products appeal to "everyone"? Very few.

Market Segmentation

Consumer Market (B to C)

Geographic factors
  Where buyers are located
Demographic factors
  Age, gender, income, ethnicity, education
Psychographic factors
  Buying motives, personality traits, lifestyle
Buying patterns
  Frequency, where purchases made

Business Market (B to B)

Location
Size
Industry

Diagram 11.1

Factors such as those identified in Diagram 11.1 have a strong influence on what a customer will buy. The initial segmentation factor is to divide the market by type of customer—a consumer market or a business market. In consumer markets, households and individuals purchase products for their own use. In a business market, the buyer is another business.

Let's use clothing as an example. I was quickly reminded that clothing is designed for specific target markets and that age is a significant demographic factor when I offered my 30-year-old daughter some clothes that I rarely wore anymore. The items were practically new, and, since we are about the same size, I was sure she would be thrilled to have them. Besides, as a young attorney with hefty law school loans, she is limited in her wardrobe budget. But as she went through the pile of treasures from my closet, only one or two items made the cut; the rest went into the Goodwill pile. She commented that some items were too long/short, the color was wrong or the style was old-fashioned.

This illustrated to me the point that entrepreneurs selling women's clothing would be out of business quickly if they thought "everyone" was their target market.

In many cases, there are several potential target markets to which you might sell. If so, your initial challenge becomes one of determining priorities, which is the "best" target market with which to start. In making this determination in Pause & Reflect, consider factors such as sales and profit potential, the competitive environment in each market and your ability to reach the market.

To identify your primary target market more specifically, complete Action Step 11.2.

Pause & Reflect
What is your primary target market and why was it chosen?

11.2 ACTION STEP
primary target market

Is your **primary** target market a consumer or business market? Depending on which, answer the appropriate list of questions below.

Consumer Market		Business Market	
Questions	Your Answers	Questions	Your Answers
For potential customers:	For potential customers:	For potential customers:	For potential customers:
1. In what geographic area do they reside?	1.	1. In what geographic area are most located?	1.
2. What age and/or income range is most typical?	2.	2. In what industry are the majority?	2.
3. What other demographic factors are relevant?	3.	3. What is the typical size of business?	3.
4. What psychographic factors are relevant (i.e., image, motivation)?	4.	4. What other factors are relevant?	4.
5. What are consumers' buying patterns.	5.		

Now that you are clear on who your customers are, you can better match your product/service to their needs. But that still leaves another challenge. How will you reach your target market?

Bootstrap Marketing

Throughout this book, you've read about the importance of minimizing your financial investment while at the same time achieving your business goals. The same holds true as you consider ways to market your products and services. You'll hear terms like "guerilla marketing" or "bootstrapping" in reference to doing more with less.

Entrepreneurs become very savvy in how to get the most out of their marketing dollars. In addition to, or instead of, the traditional marketing techniques—sales calls, advertising, media and so on—many entrepreneurs have launched aggressive and very successful marketing campaigns with free publicity and social networking. Read "Guerrilla Marketing for *Boomer-Preneurs* Book" for how you can help pass on the word about *BoomerPreneurs*.

Consider writing articles related to your product or service and submitting them to your local newspapers. Or write a special-interest article as a subject-matter expert to get your name and that of your business in front of the public. By the time you launch your business, you should, indeed, be an expert, and your knowledge may be helpful to others.

This was the case with our Featured Entrepreneur, Joe Padavic of Teardrop Video, on page 237. His marketing strategy included writing an article which instructed readers on how to preserve old photographs. It was featured in a magazine targeted to readers 50 years of age and older.

Guerrilla Marketing for BoomerPreneurs Book. I'm going to practice what I preach and ask you to help me with guerilla marketing efforts for this book. If you have found this book helpful, e-mail three or more of your Baby Boomer friends and recommend that they order it at consultACH.com, my business Web site, or one of the online bookstores.

Many newspapers and local magazines are looking for items of interest in their community. Your article is more likely to be published if it coincides with a calendar event or something timely. For example, when I was a partner in a trailer manufacturing company whose product line included a small trailer for transporting everything needed for sports tailgating events, I wrote an article and sent it to the local papers just prior to the first pro-football game of the season. Several local papers mentioned the product, and one featured the article—along with a color picture of the trailer prominently displayed on the front page of the local section.

If you don't have an event to write about, stage one. It might be your grand opening, a featured expert that you bring in to speak to customers or a charity event sponsorship.

Generational Marketing

Each generation has differences in how they communicate. I was reminded of this when my grandchildren offered to teach me to text message. They thoroughly enjoyed the fact that at 11 and 15 years old they knew how and I didn't. Now think about the challenges of marketing to the different generations.

Typically, people are most comfortable communicating within their own generation and up to a decade on either side. Language, points of reference, values and experiences are easily shared within this age range. It becomes more challenging when communicating with different generations. So, regardless of whether you are selling directly to younger generations as consumers or as decision makers in the businesses to which you sell, an awareness of differences is important and a complete course of study in itself.

Relate to your customers in the way **they** are most comfortable. For example, my husband and I own a rental house that we recently rented by listing it on Craigslist. In the past, we had listed it in the local paper or put signs in the yard, with varying degrees of success. The primary target market for this small home is young married couples. I was advised by one of my daughters that this market looks to Craigslist for anything from exercise and music equipment to home rentals. Without my daughter's input, I would not have thought of Craigslist.

Newer ways of reaching people, such as social marketing—FaceBook, Twitter, LinkedIn® and blogs—may need to be added to your marketing efforts. Read "U-Tube Marketing" for an example of how Ford Motor Company is marketing to the younger generations of drivers, the target market for their Ford Fiesta.

A word of caution, however. Just as with other advertising methods, marketing through social media takes time. Make sure it provides the results you want before investing too much of this precious resource in this marketing method.

It's not just about the technology you use to reach customers. It's also what you say and how you say it. If you need help reaching the younger generations of buyers, you may want to consult with a marketing professional. There are also many books on the subject of generational marketing that provide interesting reading and marketing advice. The Library of Congress Web site may be helpful:

http://www.loc.gov/rr/business/marketing/generational.
html#trends

U-Tube Marketing

Ford Motor Company provided their new 2009 Ford Fiesta along with gas, maintenance and insurance to a young Kansas City woman to drive for six months in exchange for completing a "mission" a month, documenting it on video and posting the video online. The idea is to have 100 trendsetters, mostly 20 and 30 year olds, blog about/Twitter/ post YouTube videos about their experiences with Ford's "global car." Article by Tim Engle in The Kansas City Star.

Why Will Customers Buy From You— Basis for a Competitive Advantage

To set yourself apart from others, you have to understand your customers' needs and your competition's strengths and weaknesses. Another "me too" business will not allow you to succeed at the level you want.

Business Strengths

A competitive advantage is gained by offering consumers greater value—increasing the ratio of benefits to price. This greater value is made possible because your business does something better than others in the marketplace. For example, what competitive advantage does Walmart have? Apple Computer? Starbucks? Your possible answers may include the following: Walmart—price, partly due to their extremely efficient distribution system, Apple Computer—product (creative software), Starbucks—speedy service.

Too often, aspiring entrepreneurs claim they will have a competitive advantage—lower prices, higher quality, better service—but these claims ring false or are short lived unless they are supported by specific expertise or areas of excellence.

So what can give you a true advantage? Perhaps it stems from your ability to offer an innovative product to a niche market. It may be your business's efficient distribution network or excellent customer service. Or it may be based on a unique combination of skills and talents you possess that are hard to find, as were those of my interior designer described in "Unique Skills Give the Edge."

Many times the same characteristics or skills that define your place within your peer group, work environment or family set you apart in the marketplace as well. What makes you distinctive or different? A closer look at the skills and talents you identified in Chapter 7 may help you identify sources of your competitive advantage in *Pause & Reflect*. What do you do well? At what have others said you excel? What have you received recognition for in the past?

Pause & Reflect
How does your business idea utilize your skills, interests and talents?

_____

_____

_____

_____

_____

_____

_____

_____

_____

> *"Opportunity is missed by most people because*
> *it is dressed in overalls and looks like work."*
> Thomas Edison

Intellectual Property

Your intellectual property may be the source of your competitive advantage and, perhaps, the most valuable asset of your business. It may include an innovative product, trade secrets or copyrighted materials. It may be the strong brand you create or the name recognition your business builds.

If your intellectual property is an important asset of your business, consider how you can protect it, just as you would protect any of your business's assets. Be sure to consult an attorney when making decisions regarding your intellectual property. The following is a brief overview of common methods of protecting intellectual property but is not meant to replace sound legal advice:

- **Copyright**—protects the creator's exclusive right to control the distribution of an original work of authorship usually for a limited time. As a result of the Berne Convention Implementation Act in 1989, copyright is automatic. Not registering your copyright with the United States Copyright Office, however, may have consequences in terms of reducing damages for infringement. For more information, go to the U.S. Copyright Office at http://www.copyright.gov/.

- **Trade secret**—is a process, formula, pattern, practice, design, instrument or compilation of information not generally known or reasonably ascertainable that may provide an economic advantage to a business. The classic example of a trade secret is the formula for Coca-Cola, which the company has gone to extraordinary lengths to protect. It is said that only two employees ever know the formula for Coca Cola at the same time. Luckily, such precautions are usually not necessary. Precautions such as marking materials as "confidential" and limiting access to them based on a "need-to-know" basis is sufficient in some instances. A non-disclosure agreement may also be important.
- **Patent**—is a set of exclusive rights granted to an inventor for a specific time period. The invention must be new, inventive, and useful or industrially applicable. Rights granted to a patentee in most countries prevent others from making, using, selling, offering to sell or importing the invention. For more information, go to the U.S. Government Patent and Trademark Office's Web site at www.uspto.gov.
- **Trademark**—protects the owner's use of a mark that distinguishes a good or service from others. For more information, go to the U.S. Patent and Trademark Office at www.uspto.gov.
- **Logo**—is a graphical element that, together with its logo-type (a uniquely set and arranged typeface), forms a trademark or commercial brand. For more information, call 800-786-9199 or go to the Web site for the U.S. Patent & Trademark Office at www.uspto.gov.

In the case of copyrights and trademarks, you may be able to register them yourself. With patents, likely you will need to contact an intellectual property attorney although you may want to conduct preliminary research yourself.

Defending infringement violations can be time consuming and costly as well. I found this to be true recently when some of my copyrighted material was copied without my permission. In some situations, the costs of enforcing your intellectual property rights through litigation outweigh the remedies you might receive. In such instances, the best defense you have against competitors is to offer the highest quality and best customer service in the marketplace.

A couple of other types of legal protections that may be of interest are:

Non-disclosure (confidentiality) agreement—protects against a person revealing confidential company information, such as customer data, inventions and trade secrets. Contact an attorney about the likelihood of a non-disclosure agreement affording any real protection.

Non-compete agreement—restricts a person's ability to pursue a similar profession or trade in competition against another party (usually the employer). To be enforceable, these agreements typically include a specific time period and geographic location.

In Action Step 11.3 you identify your competitive advantage in the marketplace as well as the marketing strategy you will use, being sure to incorporate bootstrap marketing techniques to get the most out of your marketing dollars.

Insight or Common Sense

Some entrepreneurs ask those with whom they share their business plans to sign non-disclosure agreements. People who are in positions where they work with scores of entrepreneurs or read many business plans will often not sign such documents for fear of being erroneously accused of being in breach of such an agreement.

11.3 ACTION STEP
marketing strategy

Answer the following questions:

a. What competitive advantage will you have in the marketplace (i.e., business strengths, intellectual property)?

_____

_____

_____

_____

b. What marketing activities will be a part of your marketing mix (advertising, promotion, publicity)?

_____

_____

_____

_____

Introduction To Featured Entrepreneur

A historic plantation location provides Belmont Events and Bed and Breakfast its competitive advantage among wedding and event venues in the Greensboro, North Caroline area. The appeal of the historic Belmont mansion reaches across generational lines as young couples choose Belmont for their weddings.

Featured Entrepreneur Charlie Adams

Belmont Events and Bed and Breakfast
Event venue and bed and breakfast

Charlie Adams now owns the keys to the castle, or plantation, that is. Growing up working with family members as share croppers, Charlie would envision the lives of those inside the magnificent plantation homes of the landowners for which they worked.

Years later, with his 50th birthday quickly approaching—his personal deadline to "do it,

Belmont Events and Bed and Breakfast

rather than just wish I had done it"—he purchased the historic Belmont mansion and grounds, a paragon of architectural talent and fine materials less than 20 miles from Greensboro, North Carolina. Although not for sale at the time of his visit in 1996, Charlie left his business card for the owner in case the property became available. Shortly thereafter, he received a call that it was for sale. His initial challenge was to restore the vintage mansion and its ten acres of shaded and landscaped grounds to the splendor of its past.

The ladies' lunches, initially offered to local patrons, eventually grew into a full-service wedding and event venue booked most weekends of the year for up to 200 guests. Among Belmont's complete services are in-house catering, florists and overnight lodgings as a part of its Bed and Breakfast, giving visitors a taste of the southern charm of the yesteryear and providing the source of a competitive advantage in the marketplace.

Not only did Charlie's dream of owning a plantation home take root in his early years, he began acquiring the skills needed to own a successful wedding and event venue early in life as well. As a teen, Charlie learned the hotel and catering business through work at a local hotel. His financial expertise came from years in the corporate world as a financial manager and treasurer for an entertainment association. Bringing in a partner with a background in the entertainment industry helped round out the expertise needed for the business.

Today, at 62 years old, Charlie is looking ahead to retirement from his job as a college professor. Belmont Events and Bed and Breakfast is an integral part of his financial future.

Charlie's advice to others contemplating starting their own business at this stage of their lives is, "Be prepared for an adventure that nothing else comes close to and memories that you'll treasure for years. Keep your wits, share your tales/stories, be a good neighbor, and never forget your faith will carry you when you can't find the strength to carry yourself."

For more information, go to www.belmontevents.com.

CHAPTER 12

Test Your Idea

Now that you have determined what you will sell, who will buy from you, and how to set yourself apart from others offering similar products and services, it's time to go live and test your idea in the marketplace. It's easy to fall in love with your idea—many entrepreneurs do—but now is the time to find out what others think of it. Talk to others or show them your product and find out if *they* love it. Today's economy is tough, and missteps and flawed ideas are not well tolerated.

Real-World Reactions

You may be like me, an internal processor—meaning, we live inside our heads, so to speak. We process information internally. If such is the case with you as well, it's likely you have given your business idea a lot of thought but haven't talked to many people about what you have in mind. If you are an external processor like my husband, you process information by articulating it. You may have shared your thoughts about starting a business with family and friends over weeks, months

Entrepreneurial Paranoia

What if you tell others and someone steals your business idea? This is a common concern of entrepreneurs and, in rare cases, a legitimate one. Take reasonable steps to protect your idea by not sharing it with individuals who have almost identical skills as yours and can easily replicate it. Also be sure to protect any intellectual property you might have. For most entrepreneurs, however, operating in a vacuum poses a much greater risk than having their idea stolen. At some time in the future, your business will go public (open its doors). At that time, everyone has access to information on your business.

or, perhaps, years. Others may be ready for you to stop talking about your business idea! Regardless of your processing style, it's now time to make a concerted effort to obtain feedback on your business in a planned, organized fashion.

Some of you may be reluctant to share your business idea with others for fear they will steal it. Although a legitimate concern, we entrepreneurs can be a little paranoid. Read more about this in "Entrepreneurial Paranoia."

Once you've decided it's okay to talk to others and solicit feedback, with whom will you talk? Family members? Friends? A word of caution. You will likely hear what a great idea you have from these individuals. Either they don't want to hurt your feelings or they feel that they are not qualified to judge the value of your business idea.

If you really want to test how positively friends and family members feel about your business idea, ask them if they would be willing to invest in it. Not that you necessarily want investors, but that is the ultimate litmus test of a person's conviction about your chances of success.

When a friend originally came to me with his idea for starting a business to manufacture tailgate and small storage trailers, I encouraged him to continue researching the idea and planning the business. When he later asked me to be one of the investors/ partners, I was taken aback. I hadn't been THAT excited about the idea. Those early words of encouragement hadn't meant that I believed in his idea to the extent of risking my own money! Finally, after considerable thought and analysis, I signed on as an investor/partner. Luckily, the investment turned out fine, but

I caution others not to mistake encouragement for conviction.

So let's look at how to gather **objective** feedback on your business. To do so, you'll need to talk to potential customers (members of your target market), suppliers, other entrepreneurs and your accountant or banker or business advisors, such as those available through your local SBDC or SCORE offices. Read how one entrepreneur would have benefited by obtaining feedback earlier in her decision making process in Seek Outside Expertise Early.

Cautiously examine all feedback you receive. Look for patterns. LISTEN carefully to respondents' inferences and emotions. It may be more telling than the words they actually say.

> *"The next best thing to always being right is to find out you are wrong very quickly."*
> John Manley

In the development of this book, the feedback I received from others was invaluable. Initially, I handed out chapters to members of my book club, a social group that meets once every six weeks or so to discuss our most recent book club selection. They closely fit the profile of the intended audience for this book.

My next "product testing" effort was with a group of peers, professionals in the entrepreneurship field—two taught entrepreneurship on the college level, one had been a director of an SBDC and the fourth was an entrepreneurship consultant with

Seek Outside Expertise Early

"I think if I had heard about the SBDC sooner and talked with them before buying the franchise, they would have told me NOT to move forward," said Carol,* the franchise owner featured on page 32. The expert advice she received through her local Small Business Development Center came too late to save her business but in time to help her and her husband close it more successfully.

With the franchise already operational, Carol's SBDC counselor first directed her to an accountant with more experience with retail businesses and later to an expert in retailing, who worked with her on inventory control. When it became apparent that the business could not be saved, Carol was then directed to a consultant who specialized in closing retail businesses. Through the assistance of this person, she and her husband were able to sell most of their store merchandise at their "going out of business" sale.

*Not entrepreneur's actual name.

whom I had worked on a number of consulting projects. Now this is where I had to put my ego on the line. But my desire for objective feedback prevailed, and I asked group members to be as honest as possible. Their feedback was invaluable in the preparation of the final content of this book.

Obtaining feedback on your business concept is a critical early step in getting started. One way to do this is by surveying potential customers. The survey format in Action Step 12.1 is a guide to ensure that you cover key areas related to your business and make the most of this opportunity to obtain feedback. In the numerous courses and workshops I have taught, this activity was, by far, the one that participants felt was of greatest value. A number of them changed their business ideas significantly based on the feedback they received. I encourage you to complete it.

> *"Basic research is what I am doing when I don't know what I am doing."*
> Wernher von Braun

12.1 ACTION STEP
concept testing—oral survey

Test your business idea by asking potential customers, suppliers, other entrepreneurs, your accountant or banker or business advisors (local SBDC or SCORE) for feedback. The more people you talk to, the better. Recommended topics:

- Product or service. Start with a brief description of your product or service and ask if the respondent would purchase it (or thinks others would).

  NOTE: If surveying potential customers, it is just as helpful to find out why individuals will NOT buy your product as why they will. Probe negative responses.

- Method of promotion. Ask how customers locate your type of products or services. For example, would they look in the phone book, on the Internet, ask others, look at ads?
- Features and benefits. Ask what features are important to the buyer and why. Ask about perceived customer benefits.
- Pricing. Ask about proposed pricing. *NOTE: Feedback on pricing helps quantify perceived value. It also helps determine if you can sell your product at a profit.*
- Demographic data. For potential customers, collect information about **relevant** demographic variables (i.e., age, gender, marital status, education)

12.1

Directions

Step 1. Complete the **top portions** (with lines) of each section.

Step 2. Identify those you plan to survey. For each respondent, make a copy of the blank form on pages 257-260 in the Appendix.

Step 3. Share the information in the top portion of each section with respondent and ask the related questions which follow. Record respondent's answers on the blank form.

A. Description. Briefly describe your product or service idea. *(Write description below.)*

_____

_____

_____

_____

_____

12.1

Share description with respondent.

Survey Question – Ask respondent

1. Would you purchase this product/service?
   -OR-
Do you think others would purchase this product/service?

2. If **yes**, continue with items "B" through "G."
   -OR-
   If **no**, ask, "Why not?"

B. Marketing Methods. List types of marketing planned (advertising, promotion, publicity). *(Write methods below.)*

_____

_____

_____

_____

Share marketing methods with respondent.

Survey Questions

1. Which marketing methods would be most effective in reaching you (or others)? *(How would you [or others] expect to find out about my product or service?)*

2. What other marketing methods would you suggest?

C. Features. List the specific parts or components of your product/service. *(Write features below.)*

12.1

_____

_____

_____

_____

_____

Share features listed above with respondent. **Survey Questions** 1. Which features are of most value (to you/to others) and why? 2. What other features would be of value?

D. Benefits. List anticipated benefits to the customer. *(Write benefits below.)*

_____

_____

_____

_____

_____

Share anticipated customer benefits with respondent. **Survey Questions** 1. Which benefits are of greatest value to you (or others) and why? 2. Are there other benefits that were not identified?

12.1

E. Pricing. Indicate the approximate price or price range planned.

_____

_____

_____

_____

> *Share anticipated price (price range) with respondent.*
> 1. At this *price/price range*, would you/others buy this product?
> 2. What is the most buyers would be willing to pay?
> 3. What factors would justify my charging a higher price (or positioning product higher in the price range)?

F. Quantity

> Approximately how many purchases do buyers make in a year? *NOTE: Omit this question if purchase would likely be a one-time event.*

G. Demographic information about respondent *(Include for potential buyers [members of your target market]).* Relevant demographic questions might include: What is your age (give ranges)? How many family members live in your household? What is your educational level? What is your income level (give ranges)? In what area of the city or country do you live? *Remember, respondents are more apt to answer questions of a personal nature, like income, if they are given a range.*

Write questions about **relevant** demographic information below.

_____

_____

_____

_____

_____

_____

_____

_____

Demographic information
Ask demographic questions listed and record respondent's answers

---

Repeat this process with each respondent you question.

Once you have completed Action Step 12.1, you are ready to refine your original business concept to incorporate what you learned. *Pause & Reflect* upon this information and answer questions listed.

You can gather even more information and feedback by converting your oral survey into a written one that can be given to a broader audience via mail or e-mail. Following is a sample survey using the *BoomerPreneurs* book as an example. Note that this survey was written for a consumer target market, not a business target market.

How has your business idea changed as a result of this activity?

_____

_____

_____

What did you learn about marketing and pricing your product?

_____

_____

_____

What would you do differently if administering this questionnaire in the future?

_____

_____

_____

_____

_____

SAMPLE SURVEY *BoomerPreneurs, How Baby Boomers Can Start Their Own Business, Make Money and Enjoy Live*

Directions
Read product description and then indicate your responses to questions 1–6.

Description: *BoomerPreneurs: How Baby Boomers Can Start Their Own Business, Make Money and Enjoy Life* is a practical guide to business start-up for Baby Boomers. The book identifies special considerations for Boomers starting businesses. The entrepreneurial strategic planning process followed includes opportunity recognition, researching the business, evaluating feasibility, preparing an abbreviated plan and getting started. It also includes action steps, entrepreneurial stories, tips and resources.

1. Would you purchase this book? ___ Yes   ___ No (If no, why not?)

2. What recommendations do you have for marketing *BoomerPreneurs*? (How would you expect to find out about this type of book?)

___ Bookstore(s)   ____ Internet   ____ Magazine article

___ Direct mail   ____ Newspaper   ____Speaker presentation

___ Other (specify)   ____ Web site

3. Review the features of the *BoomerPreneurs* identified in the Description statement at the beginning of this survey. Which feature(s) are most important to you and why? What other features would you would like to see included?

_____

4. What do you see as the greatest benefit of purchasing (using) this book?

___ Time savings (a guided approach to starting a business)

___ Convenience of being able to work through material at own pace

___ Specific considerations for Baby Boomers starting businesses

___ Information on how to identify and evaluate business ideas

___ Information on how to determine feasibility, plan the business
and get started

___ Other (specify) _____

5. The price of BoomerPreneurs will be approximately $25.95.

Would you buy at this price? ____ Yes ____ No

What is the most you would be willing to pay for this book? $_____

6. Demographics – Circle correct answer

What is your work status? (Work full time) (Work part time) (Retired)

(Thinking of retirement) (Displaced)

What is your income?	Less than $40,000	$40–$75,000
	$76–100,000	Over $100,000
What is your education?	High school	Some college
	College degree	Graduate work/degree

When disseminating written surveys, be sure to disseminate enough to ensure that you receive sufficient responses to provide meaningful information. The number of responses will vary depending on how easy it is for respondents to complete the survey, their relationship with you and their interest in the subject matter.

Action Step 12.2 guides you through the process of converting your oral survey into a written one. I encourage you to do this as the more information you have about your product and customer needs, the better.

12.2 ACTION STEP
concept testing – written survey

Follow these steps to convert your oral survey into a written one. Be sure to survey individuals in your target market.

Step 1 – Revise Survey. Based on the feedback you received on your oral survey, make the appropriate revisions and prepare a typed version that can be administered impersonally (by mail, Internet, handout). All questions should be clear, unambiguous and objective. Limit your survey to one page, if possible. Test your survey before distributing it by asking several people to complete it and provide feedback on its content and clarity.

Step 2 – Administer Survey. Identify your target market. Mail, e-mail, or hand out surveys to this market.

Step 3 – Compile and Compute Survey Results. For each survey question, record responses on a blank survey form and tally responses. Then answer the following questions:

a. What were the key findings revealed through survey answers?

_____

_____

_____

b. What can you conclude, if anything, from your findings?

_____

_____

c. How will your survey assist you in developing, marketing and pricing your product or service?

_____

_____

d. What changes will you make to your product/service, price or marketing as a result of this activity?

_____

_____

_____

Now that you have tested the market's response to your product or service through market surveys, you are ready to refine your product offering and tell others about your business. The following section on preparing your "Elevator Pitch" helps you develop an effective message to share with others.

YOUR ELEVATOR PITCH

In the entrepreneurial community, you hear the term "Elevator Pitch" frequently. The term is derived from the hypothetical once-in-a lifetime opportunity of finding yourself on an elevator with a venture capitalist and having 30 seconds to dazzle him or her with a brief explanation of your business.

Even though you may not be approaching venture capitalists, it's important to have your Elevator Pitch, your business's abbreviated story, to share with everyone from a relative at a family reunion to other entrepreneurs at networking events and suppliers, service providers, investors, partners and employees. Your Elevator Pitch allows you to solidify your business in the mind of the listener and clarifies the value proposition you are offering.

In your Elevator Pitch, present the problem you're solving and do so in a brief and concise fashion. Your Elevator Pitch is not the time for technical details or to share your extended biography. Nor is your Elevator Pitch intended to make a sale. Instead, you want to hook your audience and secure some type of follow-up—whether it's an e-mail, phone call or personal appointment. Follow these tips for preparing your Elevator Pitch from "Mastering the Elevator Pitch: 5 Tips to Entrepreneur Success," at www.IdeaCrossing.org:

1. Appear spontaneous through careful rehearsing. While the best elevator pitches will appear to be off-the-cuff, they are actually carefully written, refined, and rehearsed. Don't forget to time yourself. Commercials are 30 seconds long for a reason–attention spans wane rapidly in today's information-overloaded society. Brevity is your greatest ally.

2. The meat of your pitch should include your idea or solu-

tion upfront, like the title of a book. This is not a mystery novel, so be perfectly clear about what you do. Mention the status of your venture and explain your market opportunity and unique advantages. Then highlight your revenue model (e-commerce, wholesale, retail) and drop a name or two, if applicable. Lastly touch on your long-term vision (acquisitions, profits, investor returns).

3. Above all else, keep it simple. Maybe your product employs innovative technologies allowing pet owners to track their lost pets through synching of embedded microchips, WI-FI technologies and cell phone alerts. Put more effectively: You offer peace of mind for pet owners. This simple message focuses on the market problem, not the underlying technology.

   Reprinted with permission.

Using the principles described, draft your own Elevator Pitch in Action Step 12.3. Remember, this is your opportunity to capture others' interests and, potentially, begin the process of making a valuable business contact.

ACTION STEP 12.3
elevator pitch

Draft your Elevator Pitch now—30 seconds or less, about 150 words. *After you have completed it, practice being "spontaneous" and give your Elevator Pitch to family, friends and others.*

_____

_____

12.3

_____
_____
_____
_____
_____
_____

Review your Elevator Pitch prior to attending networking and social events and be prepared to give it when asked the inevitable question of "What is it that you do?" or "What have you been doing lately?" Here's your chance to share your story. Who knows what helpful bits of information or contacts you may receive once others hear it. Doing so myself at a recent entrepreneurial event resulted in my walking out with another potential sales outlet for my book as well as the name of an attorney for some legal work I needed done.

Introduction To Featured Entrepreneur

Blondell McNair tested market demand for her products in the safe environment of a small business incubator at Springfield Technical Community College prior to expanding into a retail location, where she designs and sells special-event clothing and teaches clothing design classes.

Featured Entrepreneur Blondell McNair

Blondell's Fashion Gallery
Clothing design and sales

Boredom was the motivator for Blondell McNair to launch her fashion design business, Blondell's Fashion Gallery in Springfield, Massachusetts, a number of years after closing a similar business in New York because of burnout. After several years working for a department store and recuperating from the strain of running her own business, Blondell said, "I'm bored." Following a move to Springfield, at 55 years old, Blondell decided she was ready to go into business again.

After launching her business initially in the Springfield Technical Community College's (STCC) business incubator, Blondell moved into a 1,000-square-foot studio at Indian Orchard Mills, a retail complex of about 60 artists—including crafts, jewelry, weaving, and art—when her business could

Blondell's Fashion Gallery

support it. In her studio, she designs special event clothing, selling her own designs and those of others, and teaches clothing design classes. Blondell also teaches design and sewing part time for STCC.

In her youth, Blondell's fashion interest was encouraged by her aunt, who told her, "If you can sew for yourself, you can sew for others." Her early customers were family and friends who came to her with requests for that special dress for a wedding, fundraiser, or celebration. Years later, as a young widow with children to raise, Blondell found that fashion was the way to provide for her family.

Blondell's customers come almost exclusively through word-of-mouth referrals as her clients are walking advertise-ments for her work. When asked how long she plans to work, Blondell responded, "another 15 years. I can't keep still."

For more information, e-mail blondell3fashion@comcast.net.

CHAPTER 13

Find the Answers

Since you don't have a crystal ball to tell you whether or not your business idea is a good one, your only option is to conduct some basic research. Research doesn't have to be difficult. Every time you google a topic, you're conducting research.

You've already begun your market research by completing surveys in Action Step 12.1 and 12.2. This is called primary research—collecting new information related to a particular topic.

In this chapter you'll learn more about primary research as well as secondary research, in which you search for answers in existing data. Secondary sources include magazine and newspaper articles, books, journals, Web sites and government publications. Read in "Market Research Led to Winning Idea" how the research Delena Stout conducted led to her unique and successful business. Similar to Delena's

Market Research Led to Winning Idea. Delena Stout, founder of Brookside Barkery and Bath (see page 69), used market research to fine-tune her original business concept. Her research revealed that her initial idea, a place to bathe dogs, was not profitable enough to meet her financial goals. Research into trends in the pet industry and her interest in the health of her own dogs led her to add pet nutrition to her initial idea of a place to bathe dogs.

experience, the information you gather through research will be invaluable to your business.

Ask People

This technique is used in primary research, which typically includes surveys, focus groups or interviews. It can tell you what people buy, why they buy, and when and how they buy. Some entrepreneurs hire others to do this type of research; others conduct it themselves, developing and administering their own surveys and conducting their own interviews.

You may have expanded on the primary research you collected in Action Step 12.1 by preparing written surveys and increasing the number of respondents queried in Action Step 12.2. You may also want to use a different technique to conduct primary research, a focus group.

Focus groups typically include a small number of members of your target market, 10 or fewer. The facilitator is a neutral third party with effective facilitation skills who asks respondents a designated set of questions and probes their answers. It's typically better if the entrepreneur is not present during a focus group, as his or her presence could influence respondents' answers. For more information on conducting focus groups, google "focus groups."

Use Secondary Sources

Although this type of research is the easiest and least expensive to gather, it has some drawbacks. First of all, it may not provide the most current data or be exactly what you need to know. Because of the sheer volume of information available, the success of using secondary sources hinges on the clarity of your research goals.

Insight or Common Sense
Start gathering information early. It's easier and cheaper to make changes in the planning stage than later.

I'm a big fan of starting my research on the Internet, for convenience and because of the amount of information available. Search engines are easy to use, and you can refine your search by using the "Advance Search" feature. Many databases are available online. Some require a subscription fee, but many are free.

Consider this word of caution, however, about relying on information obtained through the Internet. Just as with any information you obtain, carefully assess the reliability of the source of the information and look for consistency among various sources of information.

The reference librarian in the library may become your best friend in tracking down information. Don't be reluctant to ask for a librarian's assistance; that's a librarian's job. Years of experience and technical know-how typically allows a librarian to quickly locate the desired resource rather than using my Alice in Wonderland approach to finding what I need.

Plan Your Research

As with most events in life, things go better with a plan. Follow these three steps to make the most of your research time and efforts.

1. **Set your research goals**. They may be worded as goals or questions to be answered. As one market research specialist told me, "You need to ask the right questions; finding the answers is the easy part." Completing the Research To-Do List in Action Step 13.1 will help you identify the information you need.

   Obviously, some information is more critical than others to your entrepreneurial decision making. One piece that is particularly important is the potential sales for your

What is the name and contact information of a local or national trade association related to your business?

_____

_____

_____

_____

_____

_____

_____

_____

_____

_____

_____

_____

_____

_____

_____

business. In many cases, this type of information cannot be found directly but must be extrapolated from data about the sales volume of similar businesses, national and local sales numbers and sales trends.

2. **Conduct research**. Before starting, consider the types of resources available. In addition to those already mentioned—Web sites, journals, articles, government data—I highly recommend that you connect with a trade association in your field if you have not already done so. This will gain you access to their latest research as well as help you meet members, another excellent source of information. Most libraries have an *Encyclopedia of Associations,* or you can google for a relevant trade association. Now in *Pause & Reflect*, identify an association related to your business if you are not already a member of one.

Now is also a good time to visit your local SBDC or SBA office. Go to the Web sites of these entrepreneurial support organizations (identified on page 64) for a location near you. If an office is not identified, contact the district office for the closest location.

3. **Compile and interpret data.** Once you have gathered information related to the research goals you set, it is time to reflect on it with a discerning eye. Look for similarities, differences and data trends. In research, quality and quantity matter.

How much research is enough? That is a hard question to answer and one you will have to decide for yourself. Information can overcome fear. The more information you have, the more confident you will be in your decision about whether or not to start your business. There is something called "analysis paralysis," however. It's often a form of procrastination, using information gathering as a way to forestall or avoid making a decision.

Test The Waters

Now that we talked about how research should be undertaken, let's turn our attention to how it often takes place—through trial and error. And this isn't necessarily bad, if the potential financial and emotional costs (time, energy and money) are low.

Your "test the waters" research might involve offering your product or service on a small scale, possibly while you are still working in a paid job. Or it might involve selling to only a few customers initially as you fine-tune your offering and test market demand. As you process the information you obtain, revise and tweak your product or service. You also gain experience, contacts and the confidence to expand your business.

In the next chapter, you determine the feasibility of your business on a variety of levels—personal, technical, management, market and financial. The Research To-Do List in Action Step 13.1 is organized by these categories to enable you to start researching the information you will need to determine feasibility in these areas.

ACTION STEP 13.1
research to-do list

Read the items in Column 1 and then check mark whether you already "know" the answer or if you need to research it. Some items may not apply to your situation. If such is the case, leave the item blank.

13.1

Column 1	Know Col. 2	Need to research Col. 3
Personal feasibility		
• Goals and vision for your future	☐	☐
• Goals and vision for your business	☐	☐
• Risk associated with venture	☐	☐
Technical feasibility		
• Government requirements and/or local regulations	☐	☐
• Contractors, subcontractors or vendors	☐	☐
• Technology requirements	☐	☐
• Timeline for production and distribution	☐	☐
• Raw materials requirements and availability	☐	☐
Complete if you will have a production facility	☐	☐
• Size and type of facility needed	☐	☐
• Appropriate location, taking into consideration:	☐	☐
o Access to markets	☐	☐
o Access to raw materials and transportation	☐	☐
o Access to workers and management	☐	☐
o Access to customers		
Management feasibility		
• Management needs	☐	☐
• Founder's and/or founding team's expertise, experience and passion	☐	☐
• Infrastructure members—attorney, banker, accountant, technology and/or industry experts	☐	☐

	Know	Need to Research
Market feasibility		
• Customer profile of primary target market: Consumer market (i.e., age, gender, education, income, marital status, other)	☐	☐
OR		
Business market (i.e., number of employees, location, industry, average sales, other)	☐	☐
• Competitive environment	☐	☐
o Key competitors		
o Competitors' strengths and weaknesses		
• Market potential	☐	☐
o Target markets (identification of a niche)		
o Estimated profit margins		
o Potential for differentiating product		
o Ability to reach markets		
Financial feasibility		
• Sufficient start-up capital	☐	☐
• Adequate profitability to make the business sustainable	☐	☐
• Sales potential	☐	☐

13.1

Now you have your marching orders. Find as much of the information above as you can to prepare to conduct the feasibility analysis coming up in Chapter 14.

Step 3 Conclusion: Refine Your Idea and Do Your Research

In Step 3, you came a long way toward refining your business idea by looking at successful businesses already in the marketplace, identifying your competitive advantage and target markets, surveying potential customers and gathering research data. The idea you have in mind now has solidified from what you identified at the end of Step 2 in Action Step 10.4, page 135. It has transitioned from idea to concept—broader, yet more specific. Now you will capture this expanded version of your business idea in Action Step 13.2.

13.2 ACTION STEP
step 3 conclusion, your business concept

Briefly describe your business concept (i.e., product/service features and benefits, competitive advantage, target market(s), marketing strategy)

_____

_____

_____

In the next step, Step 4, you conclude the decision-making process about whether or not to start your own business and, depending on your decision, move forward with your business start-up.

Introduction To Featured Entrepreneur

Paul Coakley helps others determine the feasibility of their business ideas and launch their businesses. He offers business start-up planning and operations assistance to small and mid-sized businesses with a particular niche market specialty, health care organizations.

Featured Entrepreneur Paul Coakley

Andover Associates
Business start-up planning and operations assistance

Some people have the best of both worlds—interesting work with a steady paycheck and the challenge and rewards of having their own business. Such is the case with Paul Coakley, president of Andover Associates and professor and chair of the Business Studies Department at The Community College of Baltimore County.

Paul Coakley

Paul's current dual career track followed a 30-year executive-level career in the health care industry, where he is board-certified in health care administration. After his retirement at age 50 following a re-engineering initiative at his firm, Paul decided to put his health care administration skills and insights to work in his own business: serving a niche market, primarily small to mid-sized businesses and health care organizations in need of business start-up planning and operations assistance. "I have always wanted to help businesses grow and expand," Paul stated.

Paul and a network of other consultants, which he accesses on an as-needed basis, assist these businesses in start-up planning—including vision and mission statements and the preparation of a business plan—as well as policies, procedures, hiring, retention and compliance practices. More recently, Paul's target market has expanded to include many downsized executives, 40 percent of whom he estimates are not interested in returning to work for corporate America. Paul states, "There is a growing interest among downsized corporate executives to *not* re-enter the corporate world but to begin their own businesses. Since the economy is directly affecting the 'right-sizing' of companies, this is a market that is in need of consulting companies like mine to support them in establishing their own companies."

The success of Paul's consulting business rests on his personal marketing efforts, including speaking presentations to business, education, health care and senior groups, as well as AARP chapters, to name a few. The brochures and business cards he hands out at such events and word-of-mouth publicity from satisfied clients bring in as much, and sometimes more, business than Paul has the ability to handle. That is when his expansive network of other consultants is effectively utilized.

Speaking from both a business consulting and personal viewpoint, Paul cautions entrepreneurs to "identify an appropriate niche market." For those starting a consulting practice, Paul also points out that the administrative time spent working on your business—performing the marketing, bookkeeping and finance functions—are not "billable" to the client. He goes on to say, "So although the rate you charge may appear high, you're not necessarily billing 40 hours a week." Paul also shared that Baby Boomers interested in starting their own business need to

1. Take the time to prepare an attention-getting brochure and business card. Time and effort spent here will pay off in the long run against competitors who do not.

2. Always remember to follow up, even when you do not get the job or contract. Last minute situations could bring you back into consideration, should the original contract not go through.

3. Seek referrals from satisfied customers–the best advertising is word-of-mouth.

4. Do not fall into the trap of pricing your services/products too low. Being too low can be as bad for business as being too high. Potential clients wonder about the quality versus that of your competition.

5. Become involved with local community/civic organizations. These networking opportunities can lead to new/additional business.

Paul is 60-plus years of age, but, when asked about retirement, he states, "I don't see that in my near future. I plan to continue both my work at the college and consulting with clients for a number of years to come."

For more information, contact pcoakley@ccbcmd.edu.

STEP 4

Determine Business Viability and Get Started

Step 1 What Should Baby Boomers Consider Before Starting a Business?

Step 2 Recognize the Opportunity That's Right for You and the Marketplace

Step 3 Refine Your Idea and Do Your Research

Step 4 Determine Business Viability and Get Started

CHAPTER 14

Five Litmus Tests for Determining Feasibility

Business ideas are cheap. Think of all the ideas you have considered or heard friends and family talk about over the years. Most of these ideas never come to fruition.

This is not necessarily bad. Perhaps you didn't pursue your idea for legitimate reasons, such as insufficient capital or lack of technical know-how. Subsequently you may have even seen your idea successfully launched by someone else, as did our entrepreneur in "Idea a Winner—For Someone Else."

In this chapter, you'll examine the feasibility of your business idea, not only from a marketing perspective, which is what is considered first by most entrepreneurs, but also from a personal, technical, management and financial one. A deficit in any one area may be enough to result in a "failure to launch," an idea that never gets off the ground.

> **Idea a Winner—For Someone Else.** After spending 300 hours on the development and literature for a basketball training machine that tosses basketballs out on the court similar to the way a baseball pitching machine tosses out baseballs, Featured Entrepreneur Dr. James Sheehan could not get anyone excited about his idea. Now, 10 years later, there is a machine called DISH that does just what he envisioned and is selling like hotcakes.

Feasibility Analysis

The feasibility of a business is determined in the context of both the internal and the external business environments. The internal consists of the organization and the business founder and/or founding team. The external is the marketplace. As such, feasibility is a dynamic interaction of many variables.

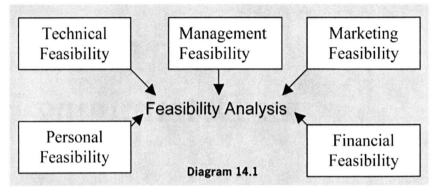

Diagram 14.1

Let's examine these areas in more depth before you evaluate your business idea on each.

Personal Feasibility

First and foremost, your business should help you reach your personal goals and your vision for the future. In Chapter 6, you clarified what those were.

In assessing your business against your personal goals, pay particular attention to whether or not your business provides the lifestyle you want. This might include work hours and schedule flexibility. For example, if you would like a schedule that permits you to travel or have time for personal hobbies, then a retail business is probably not for you, unless you have REALLY good help, which is difficult to find.

Work environment is also important and having the desired level of social interaction is a key part of work environment. If you are outgoing and enjoy interacting with people, working from home may leave you feeling isolated. Such was the case with a friend of mine who ran an insurance business out of her home. She eventually gave up her business and took a job in retail, which provided her a lot more social interaction. Working from a home office suits me well. Before my husband retired, it occasionally got a little quiet, and I talked to my dog a lot. Now quiet is not an issue.

Although these types of considerations appear minor, they can become major when you consider how much time you spend working.

Finally, the amount of financial risk inherent in the business may be a determining factor in whether or not it is feasible from a personal standpoint. Throughout this book, we emphasized that low-risk ventures are appropriate for many Baby Boomers as they want to protect their assets. Each of us is different in terms of how we access risks and how hard we are willing to work to overcome sometimes formidable odds. Whatever you do, you have to be able to sleep at night, as financial advisor Suze Orman advises in her frequent television appearances and articles.

Now reflect on how well your business fits into your personal plan in Action Step 14.1; does your business have personal feasibility?

ACTION STEP 14.1
litmus test—personal feasibility

Answer each of the questions in Column 1 by circling **"Yes,"** **"No" or "NS" (for Not Sure)** in Column 2.

14.1

Column 1	Column 2		
1. Will your business allow you to reach your personal and professional goals and create the vision you have for your future, as described in Action Step 6.1, Personal and Professional Dreams and Goals on page 75)?	Yes	No	NS
2. Will your business provide your ideal work setting?	Yes	No	NS
3. Are you comfortable with the level of risk inherent in your business?	Yes	No	NS
4. For any items on which you answered "No," can you modify your business to enable you to change your answer to "Yes"? If so, how?	Yes	No	NS
Conclusion: Does your business have personal feasibility?	Yes	No	NS

Large Quantities, Big Challenges

Dale sold hand-made fishing lures. Because of the popularity of his lures, one of the sporting goods superstores expressed interest in selling them. Obviously, Dale could not hand-make all the products, and hiring hand labor was costly. After exploring various options, including outsourcing abroad and purchasing his own equipment, which was quite expensive, he decided to forgo the large contract and continue producing the lures as a hobby. For Dale, this afforded him the best of both worlds, doing something he loved while earning income at the same time.

Technical Feasibility

This relates to your ability to meet the production and delivery requirements needed in your business. Baking a dozen pies a day is more of a hobby than a business. Ramping up production to bake and deliver dozens, if not hundreds of pies a day requires an entirely different scale of operation.

Whatever production level you set for your business is fine, as long as it fits your goals and your customers' needs. Read about the production challenges that customer demand posed to our entrepreneurs in the two vignettes, "Large Quantities, Big Challenges" and "Product Takes Longer Than Planned."

In considering technical feasibility of a product, one of your main decisions is whether to produce it yourself or to outsource production. If you produce products yourself, technical considerations include the size, type and location of your production facility.

Many entrepreneurs will not "produce" products but rather distribute them. If that's the case, your assessment of technical feasibility centers on finding quality subcontractors or vendors.

If you have or are considering a service business, (i.e., consulting, Web design, in-home nursing care) your "production," and therefore revenue, is limited by your hours in a day, unless you bring others in to help. Another way to expand sales in a service business is to add product sales to your service. Beauty salons are masters at this and typically carry a broad range of hair and personal products that their stylists sell to clients. For an example of how one chain of salons has been very effective in selling products, read the vignette, "Shear Madness Hair Cuts for Kids."

To help think through the technical aspects of your product or service,

Product Takes Longer Than Planned. The founder of a small technology business regularly attended trade shows and demonstrated the product to potential buyers, returning with a stack of business cards of interested parties. The product, however, was not in the production stage—it was still being "refined" and continued to be for months, long after potential customers had lost interest or purchased other products.

Shear Madness Hair Cuts for Kids. This is a chain of three hair salons specializing in first haircuts—cuts and styling for kids. In addition to their salon services, founder Paula Thurman reports that product sales have become a significant part of their business's revenue. "Prior to the downturn in the economy," Paula said, "the retail side of Shear Madness Hair Cuts for Kids grew dramatically, to 35–39 percent of sales. It has since stabilized at around 20 percent." Their biggest seller—toys! For more information, go to www.shearmadnesskids.com/

envision a flow chart of how your product or service originates, is produced and

finally reaches your customer. If you provide a service, envision your first contact with a customer through providing your service to the customer. Include a draft your flow chart in *Pause & Reflect*.

Then think about the equipment, tools and expertise you need to produce your product or deliver your service. Doing so will help you think through the expenses related to each activity or function identified on your flow chart. Finally, consider which of the activities or functions on your flow chart can be outsourced and which you must perform yourself. Outsourcing can be an effective way to reduce the start-up costs for your business and, perhaps, reduce operating expenses.

On the Research To-Do List in Action Step 13.1 in the previous chapter, you identified the technical information you needed and started your research. Now reflect upon the technical aspects of your business and answer the following questions.

ACTION STEP 14.2
litmus test—technical feasibility

Answer each of the following questions in Column 1 by circling "Yes," "No" or "NS" (for "Not Sure") in Column 2.

Column 1	Column 2		
List the technical expertise/skills needed in your business. _____ _____ _____ _____			
1. Do you possess these technical skills or have you identified others that do?	Yes	No	NS
2. Have you identified contractors, subcontractors or vendors that are needed?	Yes	No	NS
3. Is your production and delivery capacity sufficient?	Yes	No	NS
4. Have you identified relevant government and local regulations affecting your business?	Yes	No	NS
Conclusion: Does your business have technical feasibility?	Yes	No	NS

Management Feasibility

Do you, and your team, if you have one, have the ability to "pull this off"? Each person or team brings to the business a unique set of skills, attributes and talents. How well do they match the needs of your business?

Carefully looking at the business itself and what management expertise is needed is the starting point for making this determination. After doing so, look at your skills and experience and that of your team. What skills do you have? Do you or others have experience in the industry or a start-up situation? Can any deficits identified be addressed through bringing in additional talent or partners, hiring or contracting with others or forming an Advisory Committee?

As one investor told me, "I would rather see a grade 'A' management team with a grade 'B' idea than a grade 'B' management team with a grade 'A' idea." It's the team that determines the success or failure of a venture. If you are going it alone in your business, your team may be a loose connection of specialists with whom you contract on an as-needed basis or colleagues you consult regularly.

The following activity guides you in a review of your skills and those of your team, if you have one, to identify strengths and areas in need of development.

14.3 ACTION STEP
litmus test—management feasibility

Answer each of the following questions In Column 1 by circling "Yes," "No" or "N S" (for "Not Sure") in Column 2.

Column 1	Column 2		
Review the partial listing of business and management skills below and add any additional ones needed under "e". a. Financial know-how b. Marketing and sales know-how c. Planning, organizing and leading d. Computer skills e. Other (list those relevant to your particular business) _____ _____ 1. Which of these skills do you possess? 2. Which skills will you look for in others?			
3. Do you or other team members (if you have a team) have relevant industry expertise and work experience and business start-up experience?	Yes	No	NS
4. Have you identified infrastructure members, such as a banker, accountant, attorney, marketing or small business consultant?	Yes	No	NS
5. What are your strengths? What are your team's strengths.			
6. What skills need to be strengthened for your business to succeed?			
Conclusion: Does your business have management feasibility?	Yes	No	NS

14.3

Insight or Common Sense

Sales potential can be greatly influenced by your access to distribution channels. Those new to an industry often underestimate the difficulty of entering established distribution systems.

Market Feasibility

Will customers buy your product or service in sufficient quantities and at a price that will allow you to make a profit? That's a key question that needs to be answered.

"Anyone can sell a dollar for 95 cents."
Author Unknown

To some extent, the answer depends on the general market demand for your type of products or services and how many providers there are to meet that demand. That is, are you the only show in town or one of dozens if not hundreds? Let's look at each of these factors in greater depth.

Market demand. Look at the big picture first—the industry and how well it is doing on a national or international level. Try googling "industry outlook" "xxx," replacing "xxx" with the name of your industry. This may be sufficient to give you a general idea of where things are going. Again, market research doesn't have to be difficult.

Then focus on the smaller picture—that is, demand from your target markets within your specific trade area. Finding secondary research data related to these markets may be challenging. In some cases, you will need to assess demand by doing primary research, similar to what you started in Action Steps 12.1 and 12.2, where you survey members of your target market.

End user demand is not the only factor to consider in assessing sales potential. If you are selling through distributors or retailers, you also need to take into account how open and welcoming they are to new suppliers. For instance, in the past dissemination of books took place primarily through major publishers. For authors to sell their books to consumers, they needed an agent and a publisher. Now, through smaller publishing houses, self publishing and online retail bookstores, writers have much greater access to customers.

Competitive environment. How competitive is the environment in which you will operate, and what is the basis for competition—Quality? Price? Location? Efficient delivery? Service?

First, identify exactly who your major competitors are. Consider both your direct and indirect competition. For example, if you own a car wash, your direct competitors are other car washes. Your indirect competitors are those offering car washes as a sideline, such as gas stations and church groups holding car washes as fundraisers. Both direct and indirect competitors compete for customers' dollars. When someone says he has no competition, he usually means that he has no "direct" competition. Now is a good time to think about your direct and indirect competition and identify them in *Pause & Reflect.*

Information on local competitors can be difficult to find. A helpful Web site is www.manta.com. On this Web site, you can search by type of businesses and location (city or zip code). Information is provided by business category as well as by individual business, including revenue, date started, number of employees and contact person. To obtain information, you are required to sign up. At the date of this writing, there is no charge to do so, but be sure to check this out prior to signing up. If you own a retail business, check out your competition in your local Yellow Pages (paper edition) or at Yellowpages.com on the Internet. Your local librarian may also be able to point you to resources for information on area businesses.

In addition to the number of competitors in the field, consider your ability to differentiate yourself from others. Will the competitive advantage you identified on page 184 be sufficient?

Pause & Reflect
Who are your direct competitors?

_____

_____

_____

_____

_____

Who are your indirect competitors?

_____

_____

_____

_____

_____

Insight or Common Sense
You can learn a great deal from your competitors. They would not still be in business if they weren't doing some things right.

In Action Step 14.4, you answer eight questions about the market feasibility of your business. The research you started after completing the Research To-Do List in Action Step 13.1 will help you answer these questions. If you cannot answer them at this time, continue your research and revisit this Action Step after you have more information.

14.4 ACTION STEP
litmus test—market feasibility

Answer each of the questions in Column 1 by circling "Yes," "No" or "NS" (for "Not Sure") in Column 2.

Column 1	Column 2		
1. Is there a clearly identified target market for your product or service? If yes, describe:	Yes	No	NS
2. Does your target market have the ability to buy your product or service at your desired price?	Yes	No	NS
3. Is there a way to easily reach your targeted market?	Yes	No	NS
4. Are you able to differentiate your product/ service from others in the marketplace?	Yes	No	NS
5. Do competitors have identifiable weaknesses?	Yes	No	NS

6. Do customers perceive a need for your product/service?	Yes	No	NS
7. Does the marketplace need another provider of your product or service?	Yes	No	NS
8. Is the demand for your product or service relatively strong or growing?	Yes	No	NS
9. For items answered "NS," what information do you need to be able to answer more definitively?			
Conclusion: Does your business have marketing feasibility?	Yes	No	NS

14.4

Financial Feasibility

Put simply, do you have enough money, yours or others, to start your business and will your business generate enough revenue and profit to keep itself going?

A start-up budget can tell you what it will take to get started. A look at basic profitability gives you an idea of the kind of profit margins you can expect and, therefore, the long-run sustainability of the business. After you have this data, you can decide if the financial risks and rewards are acceptable.

Start-Up Funding and Expenditures

This is the first financial forecast you make, and it is a critical one. It will tell you whether or not you can open your doors, so to speak.

It's likely many of you are contemplating starting a low-risk venture, so the start-up costs may be minimal, as were mine for my consulting business. The example of a Start-Up Funding and Expenditures budget below is for a low-cost venture. It includes a sample of accounts in each category. Some accounts may not be relevant to your business, and others may need to be added. In our example, start-up cash is $18,000 and start-up expenses and expenditures total $10,200.

Example Start-Up Funding and Expenditures			
Start-Up Cash (list in Column 1)	Column 1	Column 2	Column 3
Equity	$18,000		
Loans			
Total Start-Up Cash (total in Column 3)			$18,000
Start-Up Expenses (list in Column 1)			
Accounting	200		
Insurance	500		
Legal	500		
Office Supplies	200		
Pre-Opening Advertising	1,200		
Printing	400		
Security Deposits			
Rent	1,000		
Utilities	200		
Other Deposits	200		
Other Expenses	1,500		
Total Start-Up Expenses (total in Column 2)		$5,900	

Capital Expenditures (list in Column 1)			
Computer Equipment	3,000		
Office Equipment	1,300		
Total Capital Expenditures (total in Column 2)		$4,300	
Total Start-Up Expenses and Capital Expenditures (total Column 2 and record total in Column 3)			$10,200

Most things in life cost more than you anticipate, so be prepared. You'll want to make sure that your start-up funds are sufficient to cover your start-up expenditures, and then some. Also consider how much of a cushion you need between start-up cash and start-up expenditures to provide the cash you need to run the business until it starts supporting itself. Getting the business started is one thing; keeping it going is another.

You may be saying, "I don't know exactly what these numbers will be." A rough estimate may do at this point. However, the more effort you put into obtaining realistic numbers, the more confident you will be in decisions based on your forecast.

Bank loans are difficult to obtain in the start-up stage of business. Most entrepreneurs rely heavily on personal savings and investments from family and friends to start their businesses. Even if you don't plan to borrow money or take in investors, you still need to project your start-up costs for your own edification and financial planning.

One advantage to being 50-plus years old is that you likely have accumulated assets that you can put into your business or use as collateral for debt financing. But just because you have these assets doesn't mean it's wise to use them in this way. Throughout this book you've been cautioned about tapping investments that could put your financial future or that of loved ones in jeopardy. Your Start-Up Funding and Expenditure forecast will help you determine if the risk is one you can assume.

Action Step 14.5 will help you determine how much you need to get started.

14.5a ACTION STEP
litmus test—financial feasibility
start-up funding and expenditures

Prepare your start-up forecast below and then answer the questions that follow.

Start-Up Funding and Expenditures			
Start-Up Cash (list in Column 1)	Column 1	Column 2	Column 3
Equity			
Loans			
Total Start-Up Cash (total in Column 3)			
Start-Up Expenses (list in Column 1)			
Accounting			
Insurance			
Legal			
Office Supplies			
Pre-Opening Advertising			
Printing			

Security Deposits			
Rent			
Utilities			
Other Deposits			
Other Expenses			
Total Start-Up Expenses (total in Column 2)			
Capital Expenditures (list in Column 1)			
Computer Equipment			
Office Equipment			
Other			
Total Capital Expenditures (total in Column 2)			
Total Start-Up Expenses and Capital Expenditures (total Column 2 and record total in Column 3)			
Conclusion: Do you have the financial resources (yours or others) to start your business? (Yes, No, Not Sure)			

14.5a

A careful review of start-up funding requirements may lead you to alter your business concept to reduce the amount of funds required. Earlier in the book, you examined ways to do so. Now may be a good time to revisit this concept. For example, if you find that the bakery or flower shop you would love to start is too costly, perhaps you can be satisfied making wedding cakes or preparing floral arrangements for weddings for a lot less money. That is, consider whether or not your business can be "down-sized" and still allow you to reap the enjoyment and profit you desire with a much smaller investment.

Your business start-up will cost about twice as much
and take about twice as long as you anticipate.
Author Unknown

Basic Profitability

In addition to having the financing necessary to start your business, you also need to be sure your business will generate enough money to both sustain itself and provide the financial rewards you want. The basic equation for determining this is:

Sales – Expenses = Net Income

This is a simple concept. It is also the basic structure of a Profit and Loss (Income) Statement, which we'll talk about in the next chapter.

The sales figure you forecast drives everything else, as most expenses are directly or indirectly related to sales volume. So how do you accurately project sales? The research you started earlier forms the basis for the sales figure you'll use to complete this equation, but additional research may be needed. For example, what is the average yearly sales amount for similar businesses in your industry?

You may be able to determine this by checking Dun & Bradstreet's *Industry Norms & Key Business Ratios* and *RMA Annual Statement Studies* by Risk Management Association. This information is organized by NAICS (North American Industry Classification System) Codes or SIC (Standard Industrial Classification) Codes and benchmarks industry ratios for large, medium, and small-size firms. NAICS is the newer classification system and lists more of the technology and service business prevalent today. To find your NAIC code, go to the U.S. Census NAICS Web site at: www.census.gov/naics. On the left-hand side of the page, enter your industry name in the space that says "enter key word"; you may need to try several variations.

Or you can try to find your codes through Google by typing in NAICS or SIC and your type of business. If this doesn't provide the results you want, think of your business in terms of its broad category, rather than specific type, to find a relevant code.

A very helpful Web site for gathering financial basics for many industries is www.entrepreneur.com/benchmark.

In addition to these various ways to locate industry and business information, I still highly recommend that you use the old-fashioned method of talking to others. Entrepreneurs running similar businesses outside of your trade area can be extremely helpful. They might not tell you their exact sales and profit figures; after all, how well do they know you? However, they will likely be willing to share average sales and profit margins for your type of business.

Similarly, other entrepreneurs may be helpful to you in estimating expenses. If you will be producing a product, you need to divide your expenses into two categories, Costs of Goods Sold (direct costs to produce a product, i.e., materials and direct labor costs) and Operating Expenses (expenses related to carrying out daily business operations that are not directly attributable to production).

Your Profitability Equation is shown here. Knowing standard mark-up and typical sales for your type of business provides an excellent starting point to project net income. Let's assume you have a small clothing boutique with sales of $300,000 the first year. Let's also assume that the cost of goods sold is approximately half of that and that your operating expenses run $9,000 a month, or approximately $108,000 for the year.

Profitability Equation

Sales

   - Cost of Goods Sold

  = Gross Income

   - Operating Expenses

  = Net Income

Your Profitability Equation would look like this:

Product Business			
Profitability Equation			
Sales	$300,000		
- Cost of Goods Sold	$150,000		
= Gross Income		$150,000	
- Operating Expenses		$108,000	
= Net Income			$42,000

Now assume that instead of having a retail store, with a cost of goods sold, you have a consulting business. Assume you generate $200,000 in income the first year. Your office expenses are minimal, and you paid yourself a salary plus subcontracted some work to a couple of other consultants for a total of $170,000 in operating expenses. Your Profitability Equation would look like this:

Service Business		
Profitability Equation		
Sales	$200,000	
- Operating Expenses	$170,000	
= Net Income		$30,000

Note, there is no cost of good sold in the above example.

If you are contemplating starting a small, low-cost venture, calculating your Start-Up Funding and Expenditures and completing a basic Profitability Equation may be all the financial forecasting you need to get started. If you are planning a business that involves greater financial requirements and risks, you will need to complete a Profit and Loss (Income) Statement and a Cash Flow Statement. You will learn more about these in the next chapter.

Again, the more thought and research you put into developing your financial data, the more confidence you will have in your decisions based on this information.

> *"Information is the key to overcoming uncertainty."*
> Author Unknown

ACTION STEP 14.5b
litmus test—financial feasibility profitability

Complete the Profitability Equation below for your first year in business and then answer the questions that follow.

Your Profitability Equation			
Sales	$_____		
For businesses producing products - Cost of Goods Sold	$_____		
= Gross Income		$_____	
For all businesses - Operating Expenses		$_____	
= Net Income			$_____
Conclusion: Does overall profitability look sufficient to sustain the business and provide the income you desire? (Yes, No, Not Sure)			

Will It Work?

Now it's time to put together the information from all the individual feasibility assessments to draw some conclusions about the feasibility of your business idea. Review your answers in Action Steps 14.1–14.5, then answer the questions in Action Step 14.6.

14.6 ACTION STEP
feasibility conclusion

Answer each of the questions in Column 1 by circling "Yes," "No" or "NS" (for "Not Sure") in Column 2.

Column 1	Column 2		
1. Does your business have personal feasibility? Action Step 14.1	Yes	No	NS
2. Does your business have technical feasibility? Action Step 14.2	Yes	No	NS
3. Does your business have management feasibility? Action Step 14.3	Yes	No	NS
4. Does your business have marketing feasibility? Action Step 14.4	Yes	No	NS
5. Does your business have financial feasibility from a start-up perspective? Action Step 14.5a	Yes	No	NS
6. Does your business have financial feasibility from a profitability perspective? Action Step 14.5b	Yes	No	NS
7. For any items checked "No," can your business be changed or altered to make it feasible? If so, how?	Yes	No	NS
8. Is your business idea a "GO" at this point in time?	Yes	No	NS

If you answered "Yes" to Questions 1-6 above, your business appears to be a "GO," but that doesn't necessarily mean you are ready to jump in and start right away. Your next step is to write an Abbreviated Business Plan. If you are seeking outside funding or your business involves substantial risks, you will then need to expand your Abbreviated Plan and write a traditional Business Plan, which is more comprehensive and includes financial projections for a longer time period, usually 3–5 years.

If several of your answers to Questions 1-6 were "No," likely your business is a "NO GO." Your Feasibility Analysis pointed out significant drawbacks to your concept. It is likely that you will not go further with planning this particular business. Even if you answered "No" to only one question, that one item may be a deal breaker, depending on its significance or your ability to remedy it. For example, no matter how good your idea is, if you can't put together enough money to launch it, that's a deal breaker—at least until the situation can be remedied.

If some of your answers to Questions 1-6 were "NS—Not Sure," additional research is needed to make a decision about whether or not to start the business.

Regardless of the outcome of your Feasibility Analysis, you learned a great deal by going through the process. This strategic planning process can be used over and over again until you identify the business you want to start. As such, you will want to read the final two chapters in this book to learn more about the entrepreneurial planning process and the next steps to take. Remember,

"If you fail to plan, you plan to fail."
Author Unknown

Introduction To Featured Entrepreneur

Gary and Sharon Duncan determined that the purchase of Frameworks Gifts and Interiors, a retail store specializing in framing and accessories, fit their personal goals and was feasible from a personal, management, technical and financial standpoint. However, they later found that their initial market assessment had to be adjusted as new information came to light, information that may have become apparent if they had done more research in the beginning.

Featured Entrepreneur Gary Duncan

Frameworks Gifts and Interiors
Retail store specializing in framing and accessories

When the corporation for which Gary Duncan worked took bankruptcy in 2001, Gary and his wife, Sharon, saw it as an opportunity to launch their entrepreneurial plans. Gary, trained as a plant breeder, had worked in executive positions in the commercial seed industry in the Midwest for over 40 years. Sharon had

Gary and Sharon Duncan

a natural talent for merchandizing, which she was able to express through her work in various gift shops as Gary's work took the family to Oklahoma, Kansas, Nebraska, Texas, Iowa and Missouri.With a good nest egg in place, the Duncans decided to stay in Missouri to be closer to grandchildren and look for a business to buy. "Sharon had followed me for 40 years as I rose in my industry and became a CEO; now it was her turn," commented Gary. "We looked for the type of business she liked." The business they found, Frameworks Gifts and Interiors, allowed them to combine their talents, his—business, hers—interior design and merchandizing—and create something special.

Today Framework Gifts and Interiors has become a renowned framing company in central Missouri as well as a great place to buy home accessories—florals and silks, candles and scents, dinnerware, framed artwork and prints, clocks, lamps and lighting, hand bags, jewelry and accent furniture. Focusing on a high-end target market, an income range of $75,000 to $250,000 or more, has allowed the business to grow over 25 percent this year, Gary commented. "We had to do a lot of adapting since we purchased the business eight year's ago," he added. "Perhaps we were a little too eager when we found Frameworks." According to Gary, this eagerness resulted in their failure to perform due diligence needed in buying the business, such as talking with customers and vendors. "Customers had changed; we didn't look hard enough," Gary said.

As an experienced top executive and SCORE counselor, Gary had preached due diligence to others, yet he didn't do enough of it himself. "We were too eager," he commented. "We wanted to live here. At first we were taken aback at what we bought. Maybe we would have still bought the business, but we would have definitely taken different steps," he said.

Gary admits that one advantage of being an entrepreneur is the flexibility to leave once in a while to see family, travel and enjoy some recreation, although the demanding nature of owning a retail shop causes Gary and Sharon to limit their travels to a week at a time or less. Many of their trips are buying excursions to Dallas, Kansas City and other regional gift markets. They visit other shops along the way to read trends and see what's selling.

Gary works 50-60 hours a week, and Sharon around 60 or more. "It's a labor of love," Gary commented. "Retail is a time eater. It is never quite done." Yet Gary says he and Sharon still have time to enjoy life—eat out and travel some—and he regularly volunteers his time as a SCORE counselor. Gary reports that their excellent staff allows them to do so. "I don't want to retire," he says. "You have to have a reason to get up in the morning."

The Duncans' business preparation involved writing a business plan along with a Cash Flow Statement, which the bank required and which Gary highly recommends to others. "Even if your plan is little more than an outline, put it down on paper," he said. Gary reported that although the property itself was collateral for their real estate bank loan, they had to pledge a portion of their investments for the rest.

There have been a number of lessons learned along the way, the most significant being the need to do research when getting started—talk to people, ask questions, get advice. "Make sure you understand what you're getting into," Gary said. He knew a lot more about the genetics of corn eight years ago than he knew about Vera Bradley handbags and Trollbeads. Now the pendulum has switched.

Gary also recommends that entrepreneurs consider their exit strategy from the time they start their business. It's something the Duncans are giving serious thought to now, with a likely exit being finding a buyer for their business when they get a little older, into their 70s.

For more information, go to www.frameworksgiftsandinteriors.com.

CHAPTER 15
Planning for Success

To be successful, a business needs a plan. It may be in your head, but nevertheless, it's a plan. If your business will be small or you are not asking investors or bankers for money, you are probably asking yourself why you would need to put your plan in writing.

The value of a written business plan is that it forces you to clarify and record what you are thinking. It is a centralized point to gather all the information you have accumulated on your business in one place and organize it into a form that is easily accessible and easy to understand. Through the process of writing the plan, you may identify gaps in information that will then guide the research you need to do prior to launching a business.

So even though you may initially question the value of a written plan, the process of preparing one is invaluable to your business's success. An article by Jason Zasky on the *Risky Business* Web site puts the benefit of a business plan as an approximate 10 percent increase in the business's chances for survival.

"In preparing for battle I have always found that plans are useless, but planning is indispensable."
Dwight D. Eisenhower

For some small, low risk, low cost ventures, you may not need the traditional long, detailed business plan that turns off some entrepreneurs so badly that they abandon writing one altogether. However, you will benefit from preparing an abbreviated version that captures the essence of the information you gathered and outlines the goals and strategies you have for your business. I call this an Abbreviated Business Plan, or Business Plan Lite. This is the type of business plan discussed in detail in this book. It is written just for you and maybe a few other close members of the team or family. This type of business plan is sufficient for many of the low-risk ventures that Baby Boomers start.

If your business requires a significant financial investment—personal savings, borrowing money from a bank or attracting investors—or involves significant opportunity costs—what you give up by pursuing your goal of owning your own business—you will want to write a full-blown business plan. If that is the case, completing an Abbreviated Business Plan is an excellent stepping stone to doing so.

As with most planning, it is the process of doing it rather than the outcome that provides the greatest benefit. By going through the business plan writing process, you clarify all aspects of your business—product/services, marketing, management and financial.

Abbreviated Business Plan

The Elevator Pitch and Feasibility Analysis that you completed earlier in this book include much of the basic content of the Abbreviated Business Plan (see diagram).

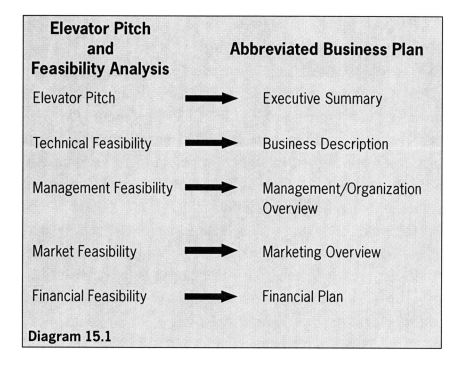

Elevator Pitch and Feasibility Analysis		Abbreviated Business Plan
Elevator Pitch	➡	Executive Summary
Technical Feasibility	➡	Business Description
Management Feasibility	➡	Management/Organization Overview
Market Feasibility	➡	Marketing Overview
Financial Feasibility	➡	Financial Plan

Diagram 15.1

In this chapter, you'll look at each section of the "Abbreviated Business Plan" in more depth and determine what additional information you need.

Executive Summary

The Executive Summary is written AFTER the rest of the plan and highlights key sections of the plan. It is your business plan in miniature.

The Elevator Pitch you wrote at the end of Chapter 12 (page 173) includes the crux of this section. Now is a good time to revisit your Elevator Pitch as it has likely evolved and changed as you completed your research. Update it and include this short

Executive Summary

Prepared after the Abbreviated Business Plan is complete.

- Brief description of product/or service
- Competitive advantage
- Market opportunity and target markets
- Owner/management strengths
- Vision for the future

Business/Product Description

- Business location and/or facilities
- Legal form of ownership
- Stage of development
- Product/service features and benefits
- Product/service liabilities or limitations
- Key suppliers or vendors

version of your business's story in the Executive Summary, along with the new information included under "Executive Summary."

Business/Product Description

Next, describe your business in more detail, including the specifics of your product or service. You have already determined much of the information listed in "Business/Product Description" by working through the activities in previous chapters. It is now a matter of pulling the information together to include here. Action Step 13.2 Step 3 Conclusion, Business Concept on page 184, is a good starting point.

Information on the various legal forms of business ownership—sole proprietorship, partnership, limited liability company, corporation or nonprofit—is included in the Appendix on pages 261-263. The form of ownership you choose has significant impact on the way your business is taxed as well as your control of the business, ability to raise capital and liability for debts and misconduct/negligence by the business.

This latter issue, liability, is of particular importance to Baby Boomers, as likely you have accumulated assets that you do not want to put at risk by operating a business. Selecting the appropriate legal structure can give you the protection you need. Now is not the time to scrimp on dollars. Consult with an attorney who works closely with small businesses on this important issue.

Management/Organization Overview

Some businesses are too small or new to need a management team, while others need a team in place from the start to seize the opportunity they have identified. In the "Management and Organization Overview," you describe who is responsible for launching and growing the business. When you completed Action Step 14.3 Litmus Test— Management Feasibility you identified key skills you or your team possessed.

Remember, a business's chances of success are based on the skills and experience of the founder and team. This section allows you to look at yourself, and others on the team, with an objective eye to identify any skills still needed.

> **Management and Organization Overview**
> - Experience and strengths of key people
> - Key positions, duties and responsibilities
> - Outside support services and advisors
> - Overview of how business is organized
> - Overview of how product/service is produced

Marketing Overview

In the "Marketing Overview," you demonstrate that your business has sufficient market potential to reach your sales goals. Let's look at each of the topics included in more detail.

> **Marketing Overview**
> - Industry—a general description
> - Target markets
> - Marketing goals (i.e., Sales? Key accounts?)
> - Marketing activities
> - Competitive analysis, including strengths and weaknesses of competitors
> - Pricing strategy
> - Distribution process

Industry. You may be very familiar with the industry in which your business will be operating as you likely have spent years, if not decades, working in it and, therefore, can easily answer questions about its growth and direction. If the industry is new to you, however, now is a good time to carefully look at it and its attractiveness in terms of growth potential. Take into account where the industry is in its life cycle (introduction, growth, maturity, decline), typical profit margins and future directions.

Libraries and Web resources often classify industry information by SIC/NAICS Codes. We looked at how to find these codes for your business earlier on pages 206-207. These codes will be helpful in finding industry information in resources such as the *Encyclopedia of American Industries* and *Standard & Poor's Industry Surveys*.

Target Markets. You began to address the topic of target markets in Chapter 11. Review your target market description on page 148 prior to writing this part of your Plan. The clearer you are about whom you are targeting, the more effective you will be in developing a successful marketing mix (sales, advertising, publicity and promotion) to reach them. Knowing who your customers are, where they live, what motivates them to buy and where they look for products will help you spend your marketing dollars wisely.

Marketing Goals and Activities. While many entrepreneurs are focused on the technical aspects of the business—producing their product or service—developing an effective marketing strategy is critical to your success. Entrepreneurs, like most of us, like to do what they know best; for many entrepreneurs, this is not marketing. Therefore, marketing is often inadequately addressed and left to the "when I get time" category.

Marketing may be where you need to stretch your wings and learn something new. In order to do so, you may want to consult with marketing experts to help with this important aspect of your business. This expertise may be obtained through free consulting from the SBDC or SCORE (at the SBA). Or you may need to hire a marketing consultant, particularly one with experience working with your type of business. There are also numerous books on bootstrap marketing—no- or low-cost ways to promote your business.

Competitive Analysis. You've already considered your competition when you looked at both direct and indirect competitors in Chapter 14 (page 199). Now is the time to more specifically look at their strengths and weaknesses. If these competitors are local retail locations, visit them. If not, examine your competitors' Web sites and talk to their customers and others familiar with the businesses. Consider how you will set yourself apart from competitors in the eyes of your customers.

Pricing. How you price your products and services is critical from both a financial and a marketing perspective. The following revenue equation emphasizes just how important pricing is to your business's success. From a **financial** standpoint, pricing is one half of the revenue equation:

$$\text{Revenue} = \text{Quantity} \times \textbf{Price}$$

From a **marketing** standpoint, pricing positions you in relationship to your competition. Will your prices be higher, about the same or lower?

Sometimes it's helpful to think of pricing in terms of a price range. The bottom of the price range is your cost. You won't be in business long if you price your products below your actual costs. Sure, occasionally you might sell a product as a loss leader, below your actual costs, to attract customers or to increase sales of other, more expensive items. But, as a rule and long term, you have to price your products above costs to stay in business.

The ceiling of your price range is what your high-end competitors charge, unless you are able to justify charging more because of some unique competitive advantage that your business has over your competitors. It might be higher quality, better customer service or a more convenient location. Without a competitive advantage that is highly valued by your

Gwen was struggling to stay afloat in her IT consulting business. After hearing from other participants in her FastTrac™ GrowthVenture class that she was pricing her services much too low, Gwen took the leap and increased her prices. Upon communicating this change to one customer, his comment was, "I wondered when you would figure it out." Her new higher prices allowed her to stay in business.

customers, they will not be willing to pay you more than what your competitors charge.

The most common error I see start-up entrepreneurs make is to price their products or services too low. Read about one entrepreneur's experience in "Customer Knew Better." I'm not sure if it is lack of experience or lack of confidence, but, either way, they are putting their business's survival at risk. Setting your prices lower than competitors' without having lower costs is typically not sustainable in the long term; it's a recipe for disaster.

An entrepreneur I know once commented that he hated "dumb" competition. By this he was referring to new companies that did not have a handle on their true costs and priced their services too low. In his case, these new competitors did not factor into their pricing the long-term costs of equipment replacement. They were able to take business away from him short-term, although they would be out of business long-term. Knowing your true costs and the prices your competitors charge will help you make an informed decision about pricing.

Distribution. Distribution relates to getting products from producers to consumers. Typically there are many steps in this process and intermediaries are necessary to promote, physically distribute and sometimes even finance the movement of products. If you are producing a product, gaining access to intermediaries in your industry's distribution chain is critical to being able to reach customers. For those of you offering a service or owning a retail business, this is not necessary as you already work directly with customers.

I realized the importance of being part of the publishing industry's distribution system with my first book, *Finding the*

Shoe That Fit. Although the book was intended for a college market and was already being used in some colleges, I felt it also would appeal to the public and decided to see if some bookstores would carry it. I found that the local branches of one of the large national chains were supportive of local authors and agreed to carry my book.

Even though I was thrilled to walk into these bookstores and see my book, it didn't take me long to realize that without being wired into the industry's normal distribution channels, which were connected to the bookstore's inventory management system, it wasn't worth my while to try to keep my books on their shelves. To do so, I had to monitor their inventory levels myself and run around town delivering books when stores were out of stock. Before writing this book, I made sure I had an efficient distribution plan in place.

Fledgling entrepreneurs often underestimate the difficulty of accessing firmly established, mature distributions systems. One question to ask others as you plan your business is how receptive members of your industry's distribution system are to new providers?

Financial Plan

You can see by looking at the list of components in "Financial Plan" that you have already made an excellent start by completing the Start-up Funding and Expenditures Statement and Profitability Equation in Chapter 14. Now, in the Financial Plan, you'll want to expand this Profitability Equation into a Profit and Loss (Income) Statement.

Profit and Loss Statement. Following is an example of a Profit and Loss (Income) Statement for a small service business.

We'll keep things simple. By doing so, you can focus on the principles involved without getting bogged down in details. See how this Profit and Loss Statement is an expansion of the Profitability Equation you already completed.

Profit and Loss Statement

Example for a Service Business - Year One

	Column 1	Column 2	Column 3
Sales* (Column 1)	$120,000		
Less Cost of Goods Sold (Column 1)	0		
Gross Income (Column 2)		$120,000	
Operating Expenses (Column 1)			
Advertising	3,000		
Bank Charges	600		
Depreciation	2,400		
Dues and Subscriptions	500		
Insurance	500		
Marketing and Promotion	800		
Meals and Entertainment	1,800		
Office Expenses	200		
Outside Services	300		
Payroll Expenses			
Wages	60,000		
Payroll Taxes	9,000		
Benefits	9,500		
Rent	15,000		
Training and Development	1,400		
Utilities	2,000		
Vehicle Expenses	3,000		
Other:			

	Column 1	Column 2	Column 3
Total Operating Expenses (Column 2)		$110,000	
Net Income (Deduct Total Operating Expenses from Gross Income and record the answer in Column 3)			$10,000

*Sales Assumptions: Consulting Project A generates approximately $6,000 per month for a total of $72,000 for the year. Consulting Project B generates approximately $4,000 per month for a total of $48,000 for the year.

Now it's your turn. Forecast your Profit and Loss (Income) Statement for your first year in business in Action Step 15.1. You can also access an online interactive income statement template by going to the SCORE Web site at http://www.score.org/downloads/Profit%20and%20Loss%20Projection,%201Yr.xls. The online template allows you to easily change data and examine the impact this has on the rest of the statement. You can also easily build income statements for various scenarios—best case, most likely and worse case.

ACTION STEP 15.1
profit and loss (income) statement

Include your forecast below. To use an interactive income statement template, go to http://www.score.org/downloads/Profit%20and%20Loss%20Projection,%201Yr.xls

Your Profit and Loss (Income) Statement
Year One

	Column 1	Column 2	Column 3
Sales* (Column 1)			
Less Cost of Goods Sold (Column 1)			
Gross Income (Column 2)			
Operating Expenses (Column 1)			

15.1

Advertising			
Bank Charges			
Depreciation			
Dues and Subscriptions			
Insurance			
Marketing and Promotion			
Meals and Entertainment			
Office Expenses			
Outside Services			
Payroll Expenses			
Wages			
Payroll Taxes			
Benefits			
Rent			
Training and Development			
Utilities			
Vehicle Expenses			
Other:			
Total Operating Expenses (Column 2)			
Net Income (Deduct Total Operating Expenses from Gross Income and record the answer in Column 3)			
*Sales Assumptions			

Many businesses will not totally self-fund after the initial start-up investment. Additional cash may be needed in the form of equity investments by the founder or investors, or through loans. Sometimes this is a result of the mismatch of sales and receipts, or sometimes it is the result of growth.

I experienced this myself when I was an investor/partner in

the small trailer manufacturing business I mentioned earlier. The business needed money to expand production capacity because of sales growth. Rather than asking investors/partners for an additional equity investment, the company decided to go to the bank for a loan. As the business did not have the assets to collateralize the loan, we investors were asked to personally guarantee it. The way the loan was structured, in case of default each investor could have been held responsible for 100 percent of the loan amount (if other investors were not able to pay off their portion of the loan). Although it was a difficult decision to make, I was not willing to take this risk, and I decided to sell my investment to the other investors who were.

Each of us has to determine what level of risk we are comfortable with and look for business opportunities that fit within those parameters.

Return on Investment. This is a good time to consider your business venture's potential return on investment (ROI). You would consider ROI on any investment, right? An investment in your business is no different.

Typically, you calculate this by determining your net income from the business and dividing it by the amount of your investment. Calculating the ROI on a start-up business can be challenging, however, as many businesses do not make a profit the first year or so.

Industry norms for ROI for businesses similar to yours may be helpful. Such data can be obtained through industry associations, by talking to entrepreneurs in the field or by looking at financial publications available in most libraries, such as *RMA Annual Statement Studies* and *Dunn and Bradstreet's Key Business Ratios*. The industry data in the last two publications are classified by SIC code.

Likely you will want to compare the ROI for your business with your other investment options, like CDs, stocks, bonds or real estate. By doing so, you are determining your opportunity costs. For example, if you invest $25,000 in your business, you cannot invest that $25,000 elsewhere. Compare your projected rate of return for an investment in your business with the likely rate of return of your next best alternative. How does it compare?

Let's acknowledge, however, that owning your own business is likely not a strictly rational financial decision. There are many reasons, other than financial, why you may want to own your own business. We examined a number of them in Chapter 3. The financial rate of return is likely only one factor that you'll consider when making your decision.

Cash Flow Projection. You may feel that a cash flow projection is not necessary. If the money needed to start and run your business is minimal and the financial resources to cover it are abundant, you may not be concerned about cash shortages. However, even the smallest businesses may have a mismatch of when money is expended and when it is received. You have to spend money to produce your products prior to selling and receiving money from your customers. As such, cash shortages within the business may occur. A cash flow projection will help you anticipate **when** an infusion of cash is necessary.

Assuming you have the funds to cover these shortages, you could make a loan to the business or an additional equity investment. With growth, however, the amounts needed increase and cash planning becomes important.

A Cash Flow Statement is nothing more than a forecast of

your business's checkbook for a set period of time, with deposits and expenditures categorized and grouped together. See the example below for a three-month Cash Flow Statement for a small service business. Normally, you would prepare your Cash Flow Statement for at least one year.

Three-Month Cash Flow Statement

	Jan.	Feb.	Mar
Cash on Hand (beginning of month)	15,000	10,000	7,500
CASH RECEIPTS			
Cash Sales	2,000	3,000	3,500
Collections from Accounts Receivable		1,000	1.500
Loan/Other Cash Investments			
TOTAL CASH RECEIPTS	2,000	4,000	5,000
TOTAL CASH AVAILABLE	17,000	14,000	12,500
CASH PAID OUT			
Advertising	800	1,100	300
Bank Charges	100	100	100
Dues and Subscriptions			
Insurance	100	100	100
Marketing and Promotion	400		500
Meals and Entertainment		200	
Office Expenses	100		
Outside services	500	300	800
Payroll expenses (taxes, etc.)			
Wages	2,000	2,000	2,500
Payroll Taxes	500	500	700
Benefits	500	500	800
Rent	1,000	1,000	1,000

Supplies (office & operating)	300		
Training and Development	200	200	200
Utilities	200	200	200
Vehicle Expenses	300	300	300
Other (specify)			
TOTAL CASH PAID OUT	7,000	6,500	7,500
CASH POSITION (END OF MONTH)	10,000	7,500	5,000

If you think cash flow may be an issue for your business, now is the time to plan for it by completing the cash flow forecast in Action Step 15.2.

15.2 ACTION STEP
cash flow statement

Prepare your one-year Cash Flow Statement on the form below or use the interactive cash flow template at the SCORE Web site at http://www.score.org/downloads/Cash%20Flow,%2012%20Months.xls

Your One-Year Cash Flow Statement												
Month	1	2	3	4	5	6	7	8	9	10	11	12
Cash on Hand (beginning of month)												
CASH RECEIPTS												
Cash Sales												
Collections from Accounts Receivable												
Loan/other Cash Investment												
TOTAL CASH RECEIPTS												
Total Cash Available												
CASH PAID OUT												
Advertising												
Bank Charges												
Dues and Subscriptions												
Insurance												
Marketing and Promotion												
Meals and Entertainment												
Office Expenses												
Outside Services												
Payroll Expenses												
Wages												
Payroll taxes												
Benefits												
Rent												
Supplies (office & operating)												
Training and Development												
Utilities												
Vehicle Expenses												
Other (specify)												
TOTAL CASH PAID OUT												
Cash Position (end of month)												

Now that you have a good sense of what it costs to start and run your business as well as your business's profitability potential, you are in a better position to consider the various exit strategies that are available to you down the road and start planning for them now.

Exit Strategy. Even though most people don't start a business with an exit strategy in mind, they should. As one entrepreneur told me, "Unless you want to be carried out the door of your business feet first, you need an exit strategy." Conventional wisdom says you will sell, fail, die or close the business.

Remember Steven Covey's principle, in his book, *The Seven Habits of Highly Effective People*, to "begin with the end in mind." This principle is one to emulate in building your business. Start with a specific exit strategy in mind.

When you no longer want to work, do you want to just close up shop? Leave the business to your children? Sell it in the marketplace? Sell it to employees? With the end in mind, your plans for exit will influence how you build your business.

Some of the types of businesses Baby Boomers start—consulting or small, home-based businesses—may not appear to have much exit potential. As one successful entrepreneur told me, "Most of the business is between my ears."

With advance planning, however, much of the expertise entrepreneurs have in their heads can be transferred to others or written down so they, indeed, have something to sell. Documentation is the key. Operations and procedure manuals add value to any business. An engineer I met who had sold his business for several million dollars commented that the reason he was able to sell for this price was that his was the best documented business his buyer had ever seen.

When you think about it, standardization and documentation are the secrets of successful franchises. Everything from rug cleaning, restaurants, and staffing companies are franchised. These same principles of standardization and documentation may be the key to building value in your business. Think about how you plan to exit your business and record your thoughts in *Pause & Reflect*.

Now it's time for you to put all the pieces of information you have gathered together in one document, your Abbreviated Business Plan, in Action Step 15.3. I guarantee that doing so will help crystallize your plan for your business, and provide the basis for making a decision about your business.

Pause & Reflect
What exit strategy do you envision for yourself?

_____

_____

_____

_____

_____

_____

ACTION STEP 15.3
abbreviated business plan

Follow the outline below to write and assemble your Abbreviated Business Plan.

Abbreviated Business Plan

Table of Contents

Prepared after the plan is complete.

Executive Summary

Prepared after the Plan is complete, it summarizes key points of the Plan.

- Brief description of your product/service
- Competitive advantage
- Marketing opportunity and target markets
- Owner/management strengths
- Vision for the future

Business/Product Description

- Business location and/or facilities

15.3

- Legal form of ownership (*Review Forms of Business Ownership on pages 261-263 in Appendix*)
- Stage of development (*i.e., concept, planning, start-up, growth*)
- Product/service features and benefits (Review Pause & Reflect—Benefits and Features, p.142. Review action step 12.1 concept testing—oral survey and action step 13.2 step 3 conclusion, your business *concept.*)
- Product/service liabilities or limitations
- Key suppliers or vendors

Management and Organization Overview

- Experience and strengths of key people (*Review actions step 8.1 entrepreneurial attributes, temperaments and behaviors, action step 8.2 entrepreneurial skills and action step 14.3 litmus test—management feasibility.*)
- Key positions, duties and responsibilities (*Review Pause & Reflect—Sketch Your Flow Chart, p. 194.*)
- Outside support services and advisors (*Review action step 14.2 litmus test—technical feasibility.*)
- Overview of how business is organized. (*Review Pause & Reflect—Sketch Your Flow Chart, p. 194.*)
- Overview of how product or service is produced. (*Review Pause & Reflect—Sketch Your Flow Chart, p. 194.*)

Marketing Overview

- Industry—a general description (*Review action step 9.2 industry analysis.*)
- Target markets (*Review action step 11.2 primary target market.*)
- Marketing goals (*i.e., Sales? Key accounts? Review action step 14.5b litmus test—financial feasibility, profitability.*)
- Marketing activities (*Review action step 11.3 marketing strategy.*)
- Competitive analysis, including strengths and weaknesses of

competitors (*Review action step 11.1 key competitors—what you can learn.*)

- Pricing strategy (*Review action step 12.1 concept testing—oral survey.*)
- Distribution process (*Review action step 12.1 concept testing—oral survey.*)

Financial Plan

- Overview of start-up funding requirements and sales and income projections. (*Review action step 14.5a litmus test—financial feasibility, start-up funding and expenditures and action step 14.5b litmus test—financial feasibility, profitability.*)
- Start-up Funding and Expenditures Statement (*Action step 14.5a litmus test—financial feasibility, start-up funding and expenditures*)
- Profit and Loss Statement (first year) (*Action step 15.1, profit and loss statement*)
- Cash Flow Statement (*Review action step 15.2 cash flow statement, if applicable.*)
- Exit strategy

Now that you have all this information assembled in one place, what do you think? Does it appear that your venture is still a go? In the next chapter, we'll talk about the next steps to take to pursue an entrepreneurial course of action. But first, let's discuss the traditional, comprehensive Business Plan that some entrepreneurs will go on to write.

Traditional Business Plan

As mentioned earlier, a traditional Business Plan is not needed for some of the small, low-risk ventures Boomers start. Completing your Feasibility Analysis and writing an Abbreviated Business Plan may have been sufficient for you to determine whether or not to pursue your business idea.

In which cases do you need more—a traditional Business Plan, an expansion of the abbreviated one you created? You will need a comprehensive Business Plan in the following instances:

- If you expect rapid growth or your business is complex.
- If your business requires a substantial amount of capital.
- If owning your own business involves substantial opportunity costs or risks.
- If you plan to raise money from outside sources.

A traditional Business Plan includes what you already have and more—more market research, financial projections, operations and management depth. In any bookstore, you can find numerous books on how to write a winning Business Plan. There is also a variety of software programs to guide you in the process. In addition, free Business Plan templates are available online, including one from SCORE at http://www.score. org/template_gallery.html?gclid=COHwr925hpYCFR8. A nice feature at the SCORE Web site is that through it you can access free online mentoring.

You can also find many sample Business Plans online, and, perhaps, one for your type of business. If you find one, it can serve as a point of reference and guide. For sample plans from the SBA, go to http://www.bplans.com/samples/sba.cfm.

Introduction To Featured Entrepreneur

Several years of running his business part time prepared Joe Padavic to "take the plunge," as he describes it, and quit his full-time job.

Featured Entrepreneur Joe Padavic

Teardrop Video
Service to preserve keepsake images—films, video tapes,
photos and 35-mm slides.

Joe Padavic looked back with regret on the thousands of pictures, and family history along with them, that were relegated to the dumpster when an elderly aunt passed away. She was a WAVE in World War II and an amateur photographer. That was when he saw the opportunity to help others preserve their cherished memories. Teardrop Video does just that. Teardrop Video can preserve customers' keepsake images in a convenient DVD format that will play in their home DVD players for

Joe Padavic

years to come. Films, video tapes, photos and 35- mm slides can all be made into Kodak moments for future generations.

Joe had a long-term goal of renovating the Michigan cottage he purchased from his parents and operating it as a bed and breakfast. In addition, he sought a business that would balance the seasonal nature of a B&B. Teardrop Video seems ideal. "So much of what a person does in retirement takes money," Joe commented. "I wanted to find something to do and earn extra money during that time."

After 35 years in the business world, working with mainframe computers and as a project manager, Joe didn't find the work fun or challenging any longer. Starting Teardrop Video while keeping his "day job" allowed him to learn the industry and market. In the process of doing so, he sought the free services of the SBDC at Johnson County Community College in Overland Park, Kansas. Every few months he met with an SBDC consultant for his "reality check," as he put it.

Over a period of several years, the video business picked up to the point that Joe couldn't continue to work full time and run the business at the same time. He had to make a decision. Joe reports that making this decision, to give up the security of a paycheck, has been his biggest challenge thus far. There was a point where he had "analysis paralysis." He kept asking himself, "Am I ready? What else do I need to know?" "It was the fear of the unknown," Joe stated, but finally he took the plunge, as he calls it, and quit his job in January of 2008.

Over the years Joe says there have been a number of lessons learned. "Early on, I should have concentrated on defining my target market rather than thinking that everyone was my customer. I tried to do everything for anybody," Joe said. "I found that two thirds of the people are not a good return on my time investment because of all the time they take. The other third are my best customers as they are interested in the benefits they will receive and are willing to pay for my services."

Joe reports that about 35 percent of his business comes from his Web site, a little from *The Yellow Pages*, and the rest from networking with Chambers of Commerce members, other "networking" organizations and referrals from family and friends. Recently Joe has begun speaking to organizations on "What You Can Do to Preserve Photos and Films" as a way to promote his business. "Organizations are always looking for guest speakers to give a 20- to 30-minute presentation," he commented.

In terms of what he would do differently, Joe sees a need to balance research of the technology aspects of the business with the business aspects. He also emphasizes the importance of working "on your business," rather than exclusively "in it," a principle he strongly advocates from the book, *E-Myth Revisited: Why Most Small Businesses Don't Work and What to Do About It,* by Michael E. Gerber, "Working 60–80 hours a week is not fun," Joe commented. "By focusing on what you do best and hiring the rest, you are able to keep work within realistic limits."

For more information, go to www.teardropvideo.com.

CHAPTER 16

Getting Started— Next Steps

You've come a long way since the beginning of this book. And by coming this far, you've already demonstrated an important characteristic of successful entrepreneurs—perseverance! That, plus your tendency toward calculated risk taking—which you demonstrated by purchasing this book prior to jumping in and starting your business—bodes well for your chances of success.

Let's look at the path you have traveled so far.

BoomerPreneurs

Step 1 What Should Baby Boomers Consider Before Starting a Business?

▼

Step 2 Recognize the Opportunity That's Right for You and the Marketplace

▼

Step 3 Refine Your Idea and Do Your Research

▼

Step 4 Determine Business Viability and Get Started

▼

Diagram 16.1

By going through the four-step process described in this book, you established goals for your future and business and determined your strengths and talents. You investigated the marketplace and looked at your business's financial requirements and funding capabilities. You conducted basic market research and evaluated the feasibility of your business through a Feasibility Analysis and the preparation of an Abbreviated Business Plan. Now it's time to take a deep breath and *Pause & Reflect* on where you are in the decision-making process.

All the statements included, with the exception of "Starting over" indicate that you are moving forward with your business planning. With that in mind, following are some additional points for you to consider early in the start-up process.

Build The Network You Need

As an entrepreneur you'll need an expanded, diverse network of people to help you launch and grow your business. This might include other entrepreneurs, service providers—a banker, attorney and accountant—potential clients and customers, experts in your industry and suppliers. As you reflect on your current network, you will probably decide that it is not the network you need to reach your goals for your business.

Start networking now, even if your business start-up is planned for some time down the road. You will access your network to find partners, investors, employees, vendors, contract workers and customers. The first time you talk with someone is typically NOT the time to ask them to buy your product, invest in your business, loan you money or give you the name of their trusted accountant. Building relationships takes time.

Consider an activity I call "targeted networking." I use this terminology to describe the process of identifying and nurturing relationships with individuals who can contribute to and support your success. One way to do so is to identify organizations or groups to which potential networking members belong. For many readers, this is an easy task as you are starting a business in a field in which you worked for years. Others who are venturing into unchartered territories will need to research potential organizations. Your research may include asking those in the field to what organizations they belong, searching the Internet and the local *Yellow Pages* for trade or professional organizations or checking the *Encyclopedia of Associations* found in most libraries. Many business owners belong to their local chambers of commerce; joining the chamber may also be an excellent way for you to make contacts.

In selecting an organization, determine if its goals are consistent with yours and if the organization is a vehicle for individuals to exchange information, ideas, support and contacts. Some organizations allow potential members to attend several meetings prior to making a decision to join.

And don't forget to make the most of networking opportunities in the organizations to which you already belong. Do you hold an office? Volunteer your time? Act as a speaker? Attend events where you arrive early and stay late to talk with others? Asking someone to meet for coffee or lunch to discuss a particular topic is a good way to begin to build a relationship.

Sometimes third parties can facilitate your networking by including you in meetings or putting you in touch with individuals by e-mail.

Who Are Your First Customers?

Networking is an excellent way to identify first or early customers. Starting a business with customers ready and willing to buy is the ideal way to begin. Not all businesses are so fortunate, however. And entrepreneurs often procrastinate about contacting potential customers out of fear, inexperience or lack of clarity on how to reach them.

Identifying early customers is critical to successfully launching your business. Within your target market, which you have taken pains to accurately identify, which customers will you approach first? In selecting them, consider which customers are:

- Most likely to buy.
- The easiest to reach.
- Most receptive to a new vendor
- Influential with other potential buyers.

Your first or early customers can help you establish credibility and, in some cases, open doors for sales to other buyers. This is where the extensive list of contacts that you developed over the last decades comes into play. Who on your list can open doors for you or act as a go-between for you and new customers? Who will advocate for your business, provide support and take pride in your success? Are there customers who are highly respected by others in the industry or community and who would be an asset to launching your business?

Developing a First Customers' Action Plan in Action Step 16.1 will help you take steps to reach important early customers. But before you do, look at the First Customers' Action Plan that Kathy Yeager prepared to reach one of her first customers. As you may recall, Kathy was featured in the vignette "Preparation and Coaching Key to Successful Launch" on page 62. Kathy has a consulting business, Contract Training Edge, LLC, in which she works with colleges to help them market and sell workforce development and training solutions to businesses in their communities.

One of the first potential customers Kathy identified was Moraine Valley Community College. She chose this college because it was relatively large, did a lot of work in the area of workforce development and had the ability to purchase her services. Kathy's First Customers' Action Plan for this particular client looked like this:

First Customers' Action Plan

Customer Name: Moraine Valley Community College

List actions to take: Completion Date: August 31

a. Research Moraine Valley Community College on the Web. Identify key decision makers and determine size and scope of their workforce development area, their possible needs and their territory.

b. Send an introductory e-mail to decision maker requesting a telephone appointment.

c. Confirm telephone appointment a day before scheduled date.

d. Make telephone call. Ask probing questions to uncover client's needs.

e. Send proposal reiterating client's needs and proposed solutions

---

Kathy followed the process identified above. She has since conducted a training program for Moraine Valley Community

College staff members and another is planned in the next six months. Kathy maintains contact with this client through regular follow-up telephone calls. She also has included them on the distribution list for the monthly newsletter she publishes electronically.

Completing Action Step 16.1 will help you focus your marketing efforts on customers who can help you effectively launch your business. Identifying the steps you will take to reach targeted customers can also help you overcome the initial inertia and fear that so many new entrepreneurs experience.

16.1 ACTION STEP
first customers' action plan

a. Identify your first or early customers, focusing on those who can lead to other customers and help you establish credibility.

	Who Are They?	Why Were They Chosen?	How Can They Be Reached?
1.	_____	_____	_____
	_____	_____	_____
2.	_____	_____	_____
	_____	_____	_____
3.	_____	_____	_____
	_____	_____	_____

b. Identify the specific steps you will take to make your first sale with each customer identified above.

16.1

Customer #1 Name:
_____

List actions to take: Completion Date_____

Customer #2 Name:
_____

List actions to take: Completion Date_____

Customer #3 Name:
_____

List actions to take: Completion Date_____

Now that you've thought about expanding your personal network and reaching key customers, what other early steps do you need to take to prepare to launch your business? The follow checklist identifies common next steps and resources to guide you.

Start-Up Checklist

The value of a checklist is that it ensures that certain important items are on your radar screen to complete either now or in the near future. Each item on the following Start-Up Checklist requires careful consideration and, in many cases, the help of experts to assist you in making the best decisions for you and your business. For items on which you will consult with an attorney, accountant or other specialist, doing basic research ahead of time can help you use your meeting time more effectively.

A number of helpful checklists on the Internet provide actual links for the information and forms needed. To find them, google "business start-up checklist." For state-specific start-up lists, add your state's name after the word "checklist." I'm partial to Web sites sponsored by either government entities or non-profit organizations as they typically direct you to resources that are free.

Pause & Reflect
On the Start-up Checklist, under the column "Due Date," identify the date by which each item will be completed.

After reviewing the Start-Up Checklist, complete *Pause & Reflect*, in which you identify timelines.

Entire books are written on some of the topics listed. It's easy to feel a little overwhelmed. But help is available to you from a number of sources.

Start-Up Checklist Helpful Web sites are included as a starting point for investigating these issues—copy each link and paste it into your Internet browser. On many of these items, you will also want to consult an accountant, attorney or expert.	Due Date
1. Choose a business name. Helpful Web site: www.sba.gov/smallbusinessplanner/start/nameyourbusiness/index.html	
2. Decide on the legal form for the business (i.e., sole proprietorship, partnership, S Corporation, C Corporation, Limited Liability Company). Helpful Web site: www.sba.gov/smallbusinessplanner/start/chooseastructure/index.html Also see Appendix page 261 for more information and consult an attorney.	
3. Choose a location. Helpful Web sites: www.sba.gov/smallbusinessplanner/start/pickalocation/index.html www.entrepreneur.com/startingabusiness/startupbasics/location/article73784.htm	
4. Check local, county, state and national requirements—zoning, permits, licensing, registrations. Start with city hall in your area.	
5. Apply for appropriate protections (i.e., copyrights, trademarks, patent). Helpful Web sites: www.uspto.gov/ www.sba.gov/smallbusinessplanner/start/protectyourideas/index.htm	
6. Establish professional relationships (i.e., banker, accountant, attorney, insurance agent, other).	
7. Tend to the business aspects of the business (i.e., checking account, business telephone, business cards, stationery, business software, insurances).	
8. Set up your office/location (i.e., purchase equipment, supplies, inventory, signage, fixtures).	
9. Determine if you need a Web site. If so, following are key steps: ☐ Determine your goals for Web site ☐ Decide who will develop it ☐ Register a domain name ☐ Develop the site ☐ Find a Web hosting company	
10. Other: list	

Sources of Help

There are many ways to access the talent and expertise of others. Consider the options described here.

Advisory Board

The start-up and early growth stages of business are a good time to form an advisory board. Even if you have a board of directors, an advisory board is an attractive option to access the talents and expertise of outside experts such as an accountant, marketing consultant and other entrepreneurs. These individuals contribute their time and expertise at no cost. Their role is just what it says, advisory.

Insight or Common Sense

Meet regularly with advisory groups and utilize their expertise to help navigate your business to success.

Breakfast or lunch meetings every few months or a couple of times a year are SOP, Standard Operating Procedure, for most advisory boards. Likely many of your early discussions will revolve around refining your product or service and identifying and reaching target markets.

Community Resources

Contact SCORE or your local SBDC, often located on the campus of a college or university. Some libraries keep lists of community resources for entrepreneurs as well. And don't forget that your local community college or university may offer entrepreneurship courses.

There is also a host of Web sites designed to assist entrepreneurs, many with forms you can download. Google "starting a business" to find them.

CPAs, Attorneys, Consultants

Many, if not most, entrepreneurs, need outside help with business functions such as marketing, accounting, taxes and payroll. For any outside consultants you use, the more experience they have with your particular type of business, the better. Now identify the resources you will utilize in *Pause & Reflect*.

Step 4 Conclusion: Prepare Your Plan and Take Action

My life's journey, thus far, has often been a case of one thing leading to another or making the most of the situations in which I found myself. I'd like the rest of my life to be traveled more intentionally. I'm sure you would also.

I hope this book has helped you become more intentional about your future, specifically as it relates to work—the role you want work to play in your life and the type of work you want to do—specifically, the business you want to start.

Terms such as "the quantum leap" or "taking the plunge" are often used to describe the jumping-off point of transitioning from thinking about and planning to start a business to actually doing so. Our featured entrepreneur at the end of the last chapter, Joe Padavic of Teardrop Video, discussed the analysis paralysis he felt prior to finally deciding to quit his full-time job to run his business. Millions of others have also taken the leap and become entrepreneurs, believing the rewards far outweigh the risks.

As Mark Towers, a guest columnist for *The Kansas City Star*, once commented, "You don't necessarily think yourself into a new way of acting, but rather act yourself into a new way of thinking." Now is the time that many of you will start acting like entrepreneurs. You have already taken the first early steps to do so by completing the action steps throughout this book. In Action Step 16.2, you will identify the next steps you will take to continue your entrepreneurial journey.

Pause & Reflect
What sources of help will you access in your near future?

_____

_____

_____

_____

_____

_____

_____

_____

_____

_____

_____

_____

"When you come to a fork in the road, take it."
Yogi Berra

16.2 ACTION STEP
step 4 conclusion, next steps

What will be the next steps you will take to move forward with starting your business?

_____

_____

_____

_____

_____

_____

_____

_____

_____

_____

Introduction To Featured Entrepreneur

Our last Featured Entrepreneur is You. How do you want your story to read? Write it here.

Featured Entrepreneur-YOU

Think ahead three years from now. What will your entrepreneurial story be? Write it here. At the end of your story, set a future date to re-read it to see how far you've come. **Congratulations!**

_____

_____

_____

_____

_____

_____

_____

_____

_____

Your Picture

_____

_____

_____

_____

_____

_____

_____

_____

APPENDIX

Table of Contents

8.1 ACTION STEP
entrepreneurial attributes, temperaments, behaviors

Step 1. Assess strength of each item. For each numbered item listed below, indicate the **degree** to which the attribute is possessed or exhibited by writing 1, 2, 3, 4 or 5 in the space provided.

Scale

1	2	3	4	5
absent	low	moderate	slightly high	very high

Attributes and Temperaments

___ 1. Creativity

___ 2. Courage

___ 3. Trustworthiness

___ 4 Ambition (high achievement orientation)

___ 5. Capacity for empathy

___ 6. Resoluteness

___ 7. Perseverance

___ 8. Internal locus of control (feeling you control
     your own destiny)

___ 9. Determination

___10. Calculated risk taker

Behaviors

___ 1. Watchful to spot the opportunities needed to start an entrepreneurial activity

___ 2. Persuasive in seeking cooperation or investment

___ 3. Takes time for reflection in order to learn from own experiences

___ 4. Goal oriented, in order to work efficiently

___ 5. Decisive

___ 6. Pragmatic, to decrease the uncertainty and flexibility in the environment

___ 7. Self-confident, in order to face success and failures

8.1

11.1

ACTION STEP
learning from key competitors

Check your local Yellow Pages, search the Internet, or talk to people to identify successful businesses offering products/services similar to yours. Then find out as much as you can about these businesses. If they are retail establishments in your area, visit them. If not, gather information through literature and the Internet or by talking to customers and vendors. Then answer the following questions for each:

a. Name of business

_____

_____

b. Description of product(s) or service(s)

_____

_____

c. What are their best sellers?

_____

_____

d. What is the business doing right?

_____

_____

e. How can aspects of the business be improved?
   (There is always room for improvement.)

_____

_____

Repeat this activity for all key competitors.

ACTION STEP 12.1
concept testing—oral survey
respondent answer form

Directions

Make a copy of this form for each person you will be surveying. Then refer back to the information you developed on the oral survey on pages 162-167 for each of the following sections. Ask respondents the questions related to each section and record their answers in the space provided.

Respondent's name_____

A. Description.

Share description with respondent.

Survey Question – Ask respondent

1. Would you purchase this product/service?
   -OR-
   Do you think others would purchase this product/service?

2. If **yes**, continue with items "B" through "G."
   -OR-
   If **no**, ask, "Why not?"

12.1

B. Marketing Methods

Share marketing methods with respondent.

Survey Questions

1. Which marketing methods would be most effective in reaching you (or others)? *(How would you [or others] expect to find out about my product or service?)*

2. What other marketing methods would you suggest?

C. Features

Share features with respondent.

Survey Questions

1. Which features are of most value (to you/to others) and why?

2. What other features would be of value?

D. Benefits

> *Share anticipated customer benefits with respondent.*
>
> **Survey Questions**
> 1. Which benefits are of greatest value to you (or others) and why?
>
>
>
> 2. Are there other benefits that were not identified?

E. Pricing

> *Share anticipated price (price range) with respondent.*
>
> 1. At this *price/price range,* would you/others buy this product?
>
>
> 2. What is the most buyers would be willing to pay?
>
>
> 3. What factors would justify my charging a higher price (or positioning product higher in the price range)?

12.1

12.1

F. Quantity

Approximately how many purchases do buyers make in a year? *NOTE: Omit this question if purchase would likely be a one-time event.*

G. Demographics

Ask demographic questions and record respondent's answers

Make a copy of form for each respondent

FORMS OF BUSINESS OWNERSHIP

Even though it is recommended that you seek the advice of an attorney experienced in working with small businesses in determining the legal form of ownership that's appropriate for your business, an understanding of basic aspects of each legal structure will help you use your meeting time with your attorney more effectively.

Sole Proprietorship. This is the easiest to form and maintain, requiring no paperwork or approvals. Basically, you are the business, and all profits and losses go to you. There are some restrictions on what can be deducted as business expenses, such as health care premiums, so the attractiveness of this form of ownership is affected by what you want to accomplish with your business. One of the major drawbacks is that you are personally liable for the business debts, which may conflict with your desire to protect your nest egg, an especially important factor for the 50-plus age group. If the dollars or potential liability is significant, consider other legal structures that offer more protection.

Partnership. No written document is required, but a partnership agreement is highly recommended, spelling out such things as division of profits, dissolutions of the partnership, and outlining duties and responsibilities.

Income and losses pass through to the partners, and they report income and losses on their respective tax returns. In general partnerships, all partners are personally liable for the business debts (all of it, not just your share) AND the actions of other partners.

Corporation and S Corporation. A corporation is a legal entity created by state law. The corporation must operate separately from you and others, and corporate money and records must be maintained separately. Failure to do so can result in corporate members being personally liable.

Requirements vary by state, but some permit one person to fill the roles of stockholder, director, and officer. To form a corporation, a charter must be filed with the state

A corporation may elect to be treated as a partnership for tax purposes (the subchapter S election). In that case, the corporation pays no tax, and the profits pass through to the stockholders and are reported on their respective tax returns. If you make such an election, your corporation is an *S corporation* or a *Subchapter S corporation.* The *S* comes from the subsection of the Internal Revenue Code, which permits this election.

Limited Liability Company (LLC). This type of business entity is designed to combine the benefits of corporate liability protection with the "pass-through" tax treatment and management flexibility of a partnership.

To form, you must file articles of organization with your state's Secretary of State. If no election is made, the LLC is taxed like a corporation.

The advantage of an LLC compared to a partnership is that, generally, the members' liability for the debts of the LLC is limited to the extent of their investment in the business. Since it is a collection of individuals, an LLC suffers from the same limitations on raising capital as partnerships. If structured as such, it can, however, require initial contributions or buy-ins by new members as a way of raising money.

Nonprofit. This doesn't mean that the business does not make a profit. It simply means that the IRS has determined that the business meets the requirement as an organization that provides a service to the community. Purposes include religious, charitable, scientific, testing for public safety, literacy, educational, fostering a national or international amateur sports competition, or the prevention of cruelty to children or animals. In spite of the approval process being long and arduous and requiring the assistance of knowledgeable experts, Boomers starting business to give back to their communities may wish to consider this legal structure.

Although nonprofits can pay fair compensation to employees, there are restrictions on distributing Net Income to officers, directors, and members.

Note: The above information should not be construed as legal advice. Check with your attorney before making decisions regarding which legal form is most appropriate for your business.

In–Text Citations

Page 1:

"Entrepreneurship Remains Strong in 2008, According to Kauff-man Foundation." *Ewing Marion Kauffman Foundation.* Ewing Marion Kauffman Foundation, 2009. Web. 10 June. 2009.

Page 16:

Price, Christine. "Occupation Directly Impacts a Woman's Re-tirement, Study Says." *Research News.* Ohio State U, 19 Mar. 2003. Web. 11 Oct. 2008.

Page 19:

Grace, Francie. "Many Baby Boomers Plan to Retire Late." *CBS News.* CBS News, 12 June 2007. Web. 29 Jan. 2009.

Charles Schwab and Age Wave. *Rethinking Retirement: Four American Generations Share Their Views on Life's Third Act, Summary of Findings from a Landmark Cross-Generational* Study. Charles Schwab and Age Wave, 15 July 2008. Web. 20 Sept. 2009.

Page 20:

Merrill Lynch. *The 2006 Merrill Lynch New Retirement Study: A Perspective of Individuals and Employers.* Merrill Lynch, 2006. Web. 20 Nov. 2008. 11.

"Older Workers 'Pushed' and 'Pulled' Toward Self-Employment, AARP Study Finds." *AARP.org.* AARP, 17 Mar. 2004. Web. 22 Apr. 2009.

Page 21:

"Kauffman Foundation Study Finds More Than Half of Fortune 500 Companies Were Founded in Recession or Bear Market." *Ewing Marion Kauffman Foundation.* Ewing Marion Kauffman Foundation, 9 June 2009. Web. 30 Oct. 2009.

Page 28:

United States. Centers for Disease Control and Prevention. "Life Expectancy at All Time High; Death Rates Reach New Low, New Report Shows." *CDC Online Newsroom.* Centers for Disease Control and Prevention, 19 Aug. 2009. Web. 26 May 2009.

Crowley, Chris, and Dr. Henry Lodge. *Younger Next Year for Women: Live Strong, Fit and Sexy—Until You're 80 and Beyond.* New York: Workman, 2004, 2005. Print.

Stein, Rob. "Baby Boomers Appear to be Less Healthy Than Their Parents." *Washington Post.* Washington Post, 20 Apr. 2007. Web. 10 Jul. 2009.

Page 37:

Bates, Karen Grigsby. "Study Highlights the Importance of Saving." *NPR.* NPR, 17 July 2006. Web. 29 Mar. 2009.

Page 41:

Charles Schwab and Age Wave. *Rethinking Retirement: Four American Generations Share Their Views on Life's Third Act, Summary of Findings from a Landmark Cross-Generational* Study. Charles Schwab and Age Wave, 15 July 2008. Web. 10 Jan. 2009. 5-6. Print.

Page 48:

Wadhwa, Vivek, Richard Freeman, and Ben Rissing. *Education and Tech Entrepreneurship.* Ewing and Marion Kauffman Foundation, May 2008. Web. 14 Jan. 2009. 5. Print.

Page 48:

Campbell, Anita. "Top 30 Most Profitable Businesses During 2008." *Small Business Trends.* Small Business Trends. 2 Feb. 2009. Web. 30 May. 2009.

Page 49:

"Small Businesses Adapt to Economic Pressures by Finding Creative Strategies to Thrive." *RingCentral*. RingCentral, n.d. Web. 20 Sept. 2009.

Page 50:

Terry, Mark. "7 Tips for Retirement Entrepreneurs." *Bankrate.com*. Bankrate.com. 13 Sept. 2007. Web. 20 Sept. 2009.

Page 57:

Shane, Scott A. "Start-Up Failure Rates Vary—Choosing the Right Industry Matters." <u>Small Business Trends</u>. Small Business Trends, 28 May 2008. Web. 20 Sept. 2009.

Page 58:

Terry, Mark. "7 Tips for Retirement Entrepreneurs." *Bankrate.com*. Bankrate, 13 Nov. 2007. Web. 16 Dec. 2008.

Page 74:

Covey, Stephen R. *The Seven Habits of Highly Effective People*. New York: Fireside, 1990. Print.

---. "Books." *Stephen R. Covey*. Stephen R. Covey, n.d. Web. 20 Mar. 2009.

Page 83:

Gray, Farrah. *Reallionaire: Nine Steps to Becoming Rich from the Inside Out*. Deerfield Beach, FL: Health Communications, 2004. Print.

Page 94:

Trevelyan, Rose. "Entrepreneurial Attitudes and Action in New Venture Development." *International Journal of Entrepreneurship and Innovation* 10.1 (2009): 1-21. Web. 9 Mar. 2009.

Page 95-96:

Nandram, Sharda, and Karl J. Samsom. *New Perspectives Gained through the Critical Incident Technique.* Nyenrode Business Universiteit, Apr. 2007. Web. 5 Jan. 2009. NRG Working Paper Ser. 07-04.

Page 118:

Bhide, Amar V. *The Origin and Evolution of New Businesses.* New York: Oxford UP, 2000. Print.

United Kingdom. Dept. for Business Enterprise & Regulatory Reform. *Supporting Innovation in Services.* Dept. for Business Enterprise & Regulatory Reform, n.d. Web. 5 Feb. 2009.

Page 125:

Popcorn, Faith, and Lys Marigold. *Clicking: 17 Trends That Drive Your Business—And Your Life.* New York: HarperCollins, 1997. Print.

"2009 Trends to Watch." *Entrepreneur.* Entrepreneur Media, n..d., Web. 15 Sept. 2009.

Page 127:

United States. Census Bureau. Chart. *Population by Generation.* Census Bureau, 2005. Web. 8 Jul. 2008.

Page 129:

Eddy, Nathan. "Five Tech Trends to Watch in 2009." *eWeek.com.* Ziff Davis Enterprise, 2 Jan. 2009. Web. 15 Sept. 2009.

Page 206:

Dun & Bradstreet. *Industry Norms & Key Business Ratios, 2005-2006.* Dun & Bradstreet, 2005. Print.

Risk Management Association, ed. *Annual Statement Studies:*

Industry Default Probabilities and Cash Flow Measures, 2006-2007. RMA, 2006. Print.

Page 215:

Zasky, Jason. "The Odds are Against You: Why Entrepreneurs are Unlikely to Succeed." *Risky Business.* Failure Magazine, 2009. Web. 15 Aug. 2009.

Page 220:

Gale Editorial Staff. *Encyclopedia of American Industries.* 5th ed. Toronto: Grey House, 2008. Print.

Standard & Poor. *Standard & Poor's 500 Guide.* Columbus: McGraw-Hill, 2009. Print.

General References

Web

Advani, Asheesh, Financing a Not-Yet-a-Business Idea, It's next to impossible to raise funds for your "brilliant idea." But our expert offers some smart financing tips," July 10, 2006. www.Entrepreneur.com

Barnes, Tim, "What makes a good business idea?" 24 November 2007, Cambridge University. http://www.cue.org.uk/files/training-day-tim-barnes.pdf

"Five Reasons to Start a Small Business at Age 50." http://www.sba.gov/50plusentrepreneur/runningbusiness/index.html

Gangaram, Singh, and Anil Verma. *"Work history and later life labor force participation: Evidence from a large telecommunications firm."* 2001. San Diego State University .http://www.retirementresearch.org/papers/abs_transitions%20retire_E.htm

Godwin, Leslie, "Working for Free Can Be Priceless: Six Ways Becoming An Expert Reduces Start-Up Risks," http://www.businessknowhow.com/startup/workfree.htm

National Federation of Independent Business (NFIB) Small Business Economic Trends, September, 2008, http://www.smallbusinessnewz.com/tag/national-federation-of-independent-business

Reinventing Aging: Baby Boomers and Civic Engagement. Harvard School of Public Health—MetLife Foundation Initiative on Retirement and Civic Engagement, 2004. Web. 14 Oct. 2008.

Wadhwa, Vivek ; Freeman, Richard; Rissing, Ben, *Education and Tech Entrepreneurship*, May 2008, Ewing Marion Kauffman Foundation http://www.kauffman.org/pdf/Education_Tech_Ent_042908.pdf

Print

"A Quantitative Content Analysis of the Characteristics of Rapid-Growth Firms and Their Founders," *Journal of Business Venturing* 20.5 (2005): 663-687.

Carter, Nancy, Larry Cox, Paul Reynolds, William Gartner, Patricia Greene, and the Ewing Marion Kauffman Foundation, *The Entrepreneur Next Door,* © 2002.

Kourilsky, Marilyn, *Making a Job: A Basic Guide to Entrepreneurship Readiness,* © 1999, Ewing Marion Kauffman Foundation.

Singh G.; DeNoble A., "Early Retirees As the Next Generation of Entrepreneurs Entrepreneurship Theory and Practice," Volume 27, Number 3, March 2003, pp. 207-226(20), Blackwell Publishing.

About the Author

Mary Beth Izard

Mary Beth Izard is a professor emeritus, entrepreneur, author and consultant in the field of entrepreneurship. She has worked with hundreds of aspiring entrepreneurs over the years and written entrepreneurship curriculum as a member of the curriculum development team for the Ewing Marion Kauffman Foundation's FastTrac® NewVenture™, FastTrac® Planning™ and Fast-Trac® LaunchPad™ programs and their college entrepreneurship course, Planning the Entrepreneurial Venture.

In addition to *BoomerPreneurs, How Baby Boomers Can Start TheirOwn Business, Make Money and Enjoy Life*, Mary Beth authored *Finding the Shoe That Fits*, which guides readers through a four-step process to identify a business idea, and the college textbook, *Opportunity Analysis, Business Ideas: Identification and Evaluation*. Mary Beth also developed and launched the nationally recognized Entrepreneurship Program at Johnson County Community College. Her entrepreneurial experience includes real estate, light manufacturing and consulting.

Mary Beth lives in the Midwest with her husband Jack and dog, Missy.

LaVergne, TN USA
21 September 2010
197898LV00006B/134/P